MW01025897

On
Design
Thinking

HBR's 10 Must Reads series is the definitive collection of ideas and best practices for aspiring and experienced leaders alike. These books offer essential reading selected from the pages of *Harvard Business Review* on topics critical to the success of every manager.

Titles include:

HBR's 10 Must Reads on Managing People
HBR's 10 Must Reads on Managing People, Vol. 2
HBR's 10 Must Reads on Managing Risk
HBR's 10 Must Reads on Managing Yourself
HBR's 10 Must Reads on Mental Toughness
HBR's 10 Must Reads on Negotiation
HBR's 10 Must Reads on Nonprofits and the Social Sectors
HBR's 10 Must Reads on Reinventing HR
HBR's 10 Must Reads on Sales
HBR's 10 Must Reads on Strategic Marketing
HBR's 10 Must Reads on Strategy
HBR's 10 Must Reads on Strategy, Vol. 2
HBR's 10 Must Reads on Strategy for Healthcare
HBR's 10 Must Reads on Teams
HBR's 10 Must Reads on Women and Leadership
HBR's 10 Must Reads: The Essentials

On
Design
Thinking

HARVARD BUSINESS REVIEW PRESS
Boston, Massachusetts

Copyright 2020 Harvard Business School Publishing Corporation

The web addresses referenced in this book were live and correct at the time of the book's publication but may be subject to change.

Cataloging-in-Publication data is forthcoming.

ISBN: 978-1-63369-880-2
eISBN: 978-1-63369-881-9

The paper used in this publication meets the requirements of the American National Standard for Permanence of Paper for Publications and Documents in Libraries and Archives Z39.48-1992.

Contents

Design Thinking

by Tim Brown

THOMAS EDISON CREATED THE ELECTRIC lightbulb and then wrapped an entire industry around it. The lightbulb is most often thought of as his signature invention, but Edison understood that the bulb was little more than a parlor trick without a system of electric power generation and transmission to make it truly useful. So he created that, too.

Thus Edison's genius lay in his ability to conceive of a fully developed marketplace, not simply a discrete device. He was able to envision how people would want to use what he made, and he engineered toward that insight. He wasn't always prescient (he originally believed the phonograph would be used mainly as a business machine for recording and replaying dictation), but he invariably gave great consideration to users' needs and preferences.

Edison's approach was an early example of what is now called "design thinking"—a methodology that imbues the full spectrum of innovation activities with a human-centered design ethos. By this I mean that innovation is powered by a thorough understanding, through direct observation, of what people want and need in their lives and what they like or dislike about the way particular products are made, packaged, marketed, sold, and supported.

Many people believe that Edison's greatest invention was the modern R&D laboratory and methods of experimental investigation. Edison wasn't a narrowly specialized scientist but a broad generalist with a shrewd business sense. In his Menlo Park, New Jersey, laboratory he surrounded himself with gifted tinkerers, improvisers, and experimenters. Indeed, he broke the mold of the "lone genius inventor" by creating a team-based approach to innovation. Although Edison biographers write of the camaraderie enjoyed by this merry band, the process also featured endless rounds of trial and error—the "99% perspiration" in Edison's famous definition of genius. His approach was intended not to validate preconceived hypotheses but to help experimenters learn something new from each iterative stab. Innovation is hard work; Edison made it a profession that blended art, craft, science, business savvy, and an astute understanding of customers and markets.

Design thinking is a lineal descendant of that tradition. Put simply, it is a discipline that uses the designer's sensibility and methods to match people's needs with what is technologically feasible and what a viable business strategy can convert into customer value and market opportunity. Like Edison's painstaking innovation process, it often entails a great deal of perspiration.

I believe that design thinking has much to offer a business world in which most management ideas and best practices are freely available to be copied and exploited. Leaders now look to innovation as a principal source of differentiation and competitive advantage; they would do well to incorporate design thinking into all phases of the process.

Getting Beneath the Surface

Historically, design has been treated as a downstream step in the development process—the point where designers, who have played no earlier role in the substantive work of innovation, come along and put a beautiful wrapper around the idea. To be sure, this approach has stimulated market growth in many areas by making new products and technologies aesthetically attractive and therefore more desirable to consumers or by enhancing brand perception through smart, evocative advertising and communication strategies. During the latter half of the twentieth century design became an increasingly valuable competitive asset in, for example, the consumer

Idea in Brief

In the past, design has most often occurred fairly far downstream in the development process and has focused on making new products aesthetically attractive or enhancing brand perception through smart, evocative advertising. Today, as innovation's terrain expands to encompass human-centered processes and services as well as products, companies are asking designers to *create* ideas rather than to simply dress them up.

Design thinking is a method of meeting people's needs and desires in a technologically feasible and strategically viable way. This chapter offers several intriguing examples of the discipline at work. One involves a collaboration between frontline employees from health care provider Kaiser Permanente and IDEO to reengineer nursing-staff shift changes. Close observation, combined with brainstorming and rapid prototyping, produced new procedures and software that radically streamlined information exchange between shifts. The result was more time for nursing, better-informed patient care, and a happier nursing staff.

Another involves the Japanese bicycle components manufacturer Shimano, which worked with IDEO to create a brand concept—"Coasting"—to describe a whole new category of biking and developed new in-store retailing strategies, a public relations campaign to identify safe places to cycle, and a reference design to inspire designers at the companies that went on to manufacture Coasting bikes.

electronics, automotive, and consumer packaged goods industries. But in most others it remained a late-stage add-on.

Now, however, rather than asking designers to make an already developed idea more attractive to consumers, companies are asking them to create ideas that better meet consumers' needs and desires. The former role is tactical, and results in limited value creation; the latter is strategic, and leads to dramatic new forms of value.

Moreover, as economies in the developed world shift from industrial manufacturing to knowledge work and service delivery, innovation's terrain is expanding. Its objectives are no longer just physical products; they are new sorts of processes, services, IT-powered interactions, entertainments, and ways of communicating and collaborating—exactly the kinds of human-centered activities

need to engage others earlier?

A Design Thinker's Personality Profile

CONTRARY TO POPULAR OPINION, you don't need weird shoes or a black turtleneck to be a design thinker. Nor are design thinkers necessarily created only by design schools, even though most professionals have had some kind of design training. My experience is that many people outside professional design have a natural aptitude for design thinking, which the right development and experiences can unlock. Here, as a starting point, are some of the characteristics to look for in design thinkers:

Empathy

They can imagine the world from multiple perspectives—those of colleagues, clients, end users, and customers (current and prospective). By taking a "people first" approach, design thinkers can imagine solutions that are inherently desirable and meet explicit or latent needs. Great design thinkers observe the world in minute detail. They notice things that others do not and use their insights to inspire innovation.

Integrative Thinking

They not only rely on analytical processes (those that produce either/or choices) but also exhibit the ability to see all of the salient—and sometimes contradictory—aspects of a confounding problem and create novel solutions

in which design thinking can make a decisive difference. (See the sidebar "A Design Thinker's Personality Profile.")

Consider the large health care provider Kaiser Permanente, which sought to improve the overall quality of both patients' and medical practitioners' experiences. Businesses in the service sector can often make significant innovations on the front lines of service creation and delivery. By teaching design-thinking techniques to nurses, doctors, and administrators, Kaiser hoped to inspire its practitioners to contribute new ideas. Over the course of several months Kaiser teams participated in workshops with the help of my firm, IDEO, and a group of Kaiser coaches. These workshops led to a portfolio of innovations, many of which are being rolled out across the company.

One of them—a project to reengineer nursing-staff shift changes at four Kaiser hospitals—perfectly illustrates both the broader nature of innovation "products" and the value of a holistic design approach. The core project team included a strategist (formerly

need to run this programmatically

that go beyond and dramatically improve on existing alternatives. (See Roger Martin's *The Opposable Mind: How Successful Leaders Win Through Integrative Thinking.*)

Optimism

They assume that no matter how challenging the constraints of a given problem, at least one potential solution is better than the existing alternatives.

Experimentalism

Significant innovations don't come from incremental tweaks. Design thinkers pose questions and explore constraints in creative ways that proceed in entirely new directions.

Collaboration

The increasing complexity of products, services, and experiences has replaced the myth of the lone creative genius with the reality of the enthusiastic interdisciplinary collaborator. The best design thinkers don't simply work alongside other disciplines; many of them have significant experience in more than one. At IDEO we employ people who are engineers *and* marketers, anthropologists *and* industrial designers, architects *and* psychologists.

a nurse), an organizational-development specialist, a technology expert, a process designer, a union representative, and designers from IDEO. This group worked with innovation teams of frontline practitioners in each of the four hospitals.

During the earliest phase of the project, the core team collaborated with nurses to identify a number of problems in the way shift changes occurred. Chief among these was the fact that nurses routinely spent the first 45 minutes of each shift at the nurses' station debriefing the departing shift about the status of patients. Their methods of information exchange were different in every hospital, ranging from recorded dictation to face-to-face conversations. And they compiled the information they needed to serve patients in a variety of ways—scrawling quick notes on the back of any available scrap of paper, for example, or even on their scrubs. Despite a significant investment of time, the nurses often failed to learn some of the things that mattered most to patients, such as how they had

Reflecting on Design Thinking

by Tim Brown

FOR ME THE WORD "REFLECTING" in the title of this piece has a two-fold meaning. It's a privilege to reflect on the influence of my 2008 HBR article, "Design Thinking," a decade later, and it's also inherent in the practice of design thinking to reflect on and act upon what's been learned from the application of this set of tools, methods, and mindsets. While an exhaustive survey of the lessons of many years is impossible, clear patterns and insights have emerged that might be useful to those engaging with the topic today.

I didn't create the term "design thinking"; indeed, it surfaced several decades before I wrote the article. Yet there was clearly a pent-up demand for an approach to innovation that was accessible to a wider range of people in business and in society. The surprise for me was the extent of that demand. There has been a dramatic proliferation of corporate design teams over the past decade. Technology companies like IBM, SAP, Facebook, Google, and Airbnb are the most obvious examples, but sectors such as financial services and health care have also seen a surge in innovation teams centered around design thinking and powered by an understanding of what people want and need in their lives. What's more, there is clear evidence that students see a workplace demand for these skills as the number of business schools and other academic departments, as well as online platforms, now offering courses in design thinking skyrockets.

Although the core tenets of design thinking have not changed since 2008, the effects of digital transformation and cutting-edge software—artificially intelligent or otherwise—have accelerated the speed at which we can employ its methods. Our tools for inspiration have been dramatically expanded by social networks and methods for gathering data about human behavior. Similarly, we can express ideas and build prototypes far faster and at greater scale using digital technology.

In the domain of implementation, agile software development practices have transformed our expectations of what we can build and how quickly we can build it. Indeed, there is much discussion about the overlaps between agile and design thinking, and while I agree that they borrow from each other and are complementary, the distinctions between them continue to be a point of confusion and should be reiterated: Agile is focused entirely on rapid and effective implementation, while design thinking is intended to facilitate exploration *and* implementation.

While technology has undoubtedly added fuel to the design-thinking movement, it has also been the cause of some of its greatest challenges. The dehumanizing potential of technology has become only more apparent with the rise of AI. Ubiquitous social networks have fractured society as much as they have connected it. Online advertising and targeted marketing have raised rates of consumption just as the planetary damage caused by overconsumption is becoming all too clear.

Today, those who seek to use design thinking to innovate are faced with challenging moral and ethical dilemmas. Is it acceptable to use design to make a product or service more appealing if that product has clear societal downsides? The social isolation that results from the addictive power of endless media feeds, never mind the increased effectiveness of fake news, have been exacerbated by good design. Similarly, excellent design has helped to build brands that make vaping highly desirable to young and vulnerable consumers. Design thinking, like any powerful tool, comes with a duty to use it responsibly.

In the original article I posited that Thomas Edison, one of design thinking's forebearers, intuitively understood the power of systems and the need to innovate at the systems level. Today's innovators would do well to emulate Edison as they consider new initiatives. The kinds of significant problems that I hoped design thinkers would have the confidence to tackle remain significant problems today. The challenges of improving access to health care, education, and learning, mitigating income disparity, and remediating the effects of climate change and resource depletion are still far from being resolved, and some have gotten dramatically worse. There are glimmers of hope, however. In health care we have examples such as Omada Health that offer a renewed focus on empowering patients to take control of more of their own health outcomes and a more holistic approach to care. In education we are seeing examples such as Innova Schools that have designed new teaching models that give access to higher-quality learning experiences at lower cost through the imaginative blending of technology and human-based approaches. These two companies, both designed at IDEO, show that design thinking has been the source of solutions that make a difference. But there is far more to do. Personally, I find this inspiring rather than depressing. It illustrates to me that this is no time to give up on the power of design thinking but instead to refocus our energy on making these approaches as effective as possible and available to all.

(continued)

Reflecting on Design Thinking

This leads me to my final reflection: Design thinking is not easy. While this may seem blindingly obvious, it has also been a significant obstacle to many of those who have attempted to integrate design thinking into their organizations and work practices. The skills, frameworks, and procedures associated with design thinking are complex and are rarely applied effectively on the first attempt. Like so many of our most meaningful human skills—playing a musical instrument, for example, or building strong and deep relationships with other people—becoming proficient in design thinking takes time and hard work. This focus on mastery is not something we pay much attention to in today's organizations. We expect to be able to flick a switch or fire up an algorithm and instantly see results. Too many people who could benefit the most from acquiring the skills that comprise design thinking give up before they reach a level of mastery that produces a meaningful impact.

Even so, I've seen countless success stories, such as Dr. Bon Ku, an emergency medicine physician in Philadelphia, who has consistently applied design thinking to the challenge of providing health care to disadvantaged communities. I have observed engineers who have learned how to bring a deeper understanding of human behavior to their innovation. Business leaders who have become skilled in presenting compelling stories about change without resorting to PowerPoint. Teams that have created customer-centered innovations that challenge the organizational status quo and achieve significant market impact.

These are merely a few examples of those who have persevered and reaped the benefits of design thinking. The concerted, sustained effort they put toward gaining mastery brings us back to Edison once more: "Innovation is 1% inspiration and 99% perspiration." The same is true about learning to be a great design thinker. Even though expertise is often its own intrinsic reward, I challenge you to sweat figuratively and literally as you apply design thinking to the most important challenges of our time. In so doing, you'll discover the double fulfillment of achieving design-thinking mastery while you contribute to making the world better for those who follow.

---

fared during the previous shift, which family members were with them, and whether or not certain tests or therapies had been administered. For many patients, the team learned, each shift change felt like a hole in their care. Using the insights gleaned from observing these important times of transition, the innovation teams explored potential solutions through brainstorming and rapid prototyping.

(Prototypes of a service innovation will of course not be physical, but they must be tangible. Because pictures help us understand what is learned through prototyping, we often videotape the performance of prototyped services, as we did at Kaiser.)

Prototyping doesn't have to be complex and expensive. In another health care project, IDEO helped a group of surgeons develop a new device for sinus surgery. As the surgeons described the ideal physical characteristics of the instrument, one of the designers grabbed a whiteboard marker, a film canister, and a clothespin and taped them together. "Do you mean like this?" he asked. With his rudimentary prototype in hand, the surgeons were able to be much more precise about what the ultimate design should accomplish.

Prototypes should command only as much time, effort, and investment as are needed to generate useful feedback and evolve an idea. The more "finished" a prototype seems, the less likely its creators will be to pay attention to and profit from feedback. The goal of prototyping isn't to finish. It is to learn about the strengths and weaknesses of the idea and to identify new directions that further prototypes might take.

The design that emerged for shift changes had nurses passing on information in front of the patient rather than at the nurses' station. In only a week the team built a working prototype that included new procedures and some simple software with which nurses could call up previous shift-change notes and add new ones. They could input patient information throughout a shift rather than scrambling at the end to pass it on. The software collated the data in a simple format customized for each nurse at the start of a shift. The result was both higher-quality knowledge transfer and reduced prep time, permitting much earlier and better-informed contact with patients.

As Kaiser measured the impact of this change over time, it learned that the mean interval between a nurse's arrival and first interaction with a patient had been more than halved, adding a huge amount of nursing time across the four hospitals. Perhaps just as important was the effect on the quality of the nurses' work experience. One nurse commented, "I'm an hour ahead, and I've only been here 45 minutes." Another said, "[This is the] first time I've ever made it out of here at the end of my shift."

Thus did a group of nurses significantly improve their patients' experience while also improving their own job satisfaction and productivity. By applying a human-centered design methodology, they were able to create a relatively small process innovation that produced an outsize impact. The new shift changes are being rolled out across the Kaiser system, and the capacity to reliably record critical patient information is being integrated into an electronic medical records initiative at the company.

What might happen at Kaiser if every nurse, doctor, and administrator in every hospital felt empowered to tackle problems the way this group did? To find out, Kaiser has created the Garfield Innovation Center, which is run by Kaiser's original core team and acts as a consultancy to the entire organization. The center's mission is to pursue innovation that enhances the patient experience and, more broadly, to envision Kaiser's "hospital of the future." It is introducing tools for design thinking across the Kaiser system.

How Design Thinking Happens

The myth of creative genius is resilient: We believe that great ideas pop fully formed out of brilliant minds, in feats of imagination well beyond the abilities of mere mortals. But what the Kaiser nursing team accomplished was neither a sudden breakthrough nor the lightning strike of genius; it was the result of hard work augmented by a creative human-centered discovery process and followed by iterative cycles of prototyping, testing, and refinement.

The design process is best described metaphorically as a system of spaces rather than a predefined series of orderly steps. The spaces demarcate different sorts of related activities that together form the continuum of innovation. Design thinking can feel chaotic to those experiencing it for the first time. But over the life of a project participants come to see—as they did at Kaiser—that the process makes sense and achieves results, even though its architecture differs from the linear, milestone-based processes typical of other kinds of business activities.

Design projects must ultimately pass through three spaces (see the exhibit "Inspiration, ideation, implementation"). We label these "inspiration," for the circumstances (be they a problem, an opportunity, or both) that motivate the search for solutions; "ideation," for the process of generating, developing, and testing ideas that may lead to solutions; and "implementation," for the charting of a path to market. Projects will loop back through these spaces—particularly the first two—more than once as ideas are refined and new directions taken.

Sometimes the trigger for a project is leadership's recognition of a serious change in business fortunes. In 2004 Shimano, a Japanese manufacturer of bicycle components, faced flattening growth in its traditional high-end road-racing and mountain-bike segments in the United States. The company had always relied on technology innovations to drive its growth and naturally tried to predict where the next one might come from. This time Shimano thought a high-end casual bike that appealed to boomers would be an interesting area to explore. IDEO was invited to collaborate on the project.

During the inspiration phase, an interdisciplinary team of IDEO and Shimano people—designers, behavioral scientists, marketers, and engineers—worked to identify appropriate constraints for the project. The team began with a hunch that it should focus more broadly than on the high-end market, which might prove to be neither the only nor even the best source of new growth. So it set out to learn why 90% of American adults don't ride bikes. Looking for new ways to think about the problem, the team members spent time with all kinds of consumers. They discovered that nearly everyone they met rode a bike as a child and had happy memories of doing so. They also discovered that many Americans are intimidated by cycling today—by the retail experience (including the young, Lycra-clad athletes who serve as sales staff in most independent bike stores); by the complexity and cost of the bikes, accessories, and specialized clothing; by the danger of cycling on roads not designed for bicycles; and by the demands of maintaining a technically sophisticated bike that is ridden infrequently.

Implementation

3

Move on to the
next project—repeat

Make the case to
the business—
spread the word

Help marketing
design a communi-
cation strategy

Execute the Vision
Engineer the experience

Prototype some more,
test with users, test
internally

Communicate
internally—don't work
in the dark!

Tell more stories (they
keep ideas alive)

Prototype, test,
prototype, test ...

Apply integrative
thinking

Put customers in
the midst of every-
thing; describe their
journeys

Build creative frameworks
(order out of chaos)

Make many sketches,
concoct scenarios

Brainstorm

Ideation

2

Inspiration

Expect Success

Build implementation
resources into your plan

What's the business problem? Where's the opportunity? What has changed (or soon may change)?

Look at the world:
Observe what people do,
how they think, what they
need and want

Involve many disciplines
from the start (e.g., engineering & marketing)

What are the business constraints (time, lack of resources, impoverished customer base, shrinking market)?

Pay close attention to
"extreme" users such as
children or the elderly

Have a project room
where you can share
insights, tell stories

Are valuable ideas, assets, and expertise hiding
inside the business?

How can new
technology help?

Organize information and
synthesize possibilities
(tell more stories!)

This human-centered exploration—which took its insights from people outside Shimano's core customer base—led to the realization that a whole new category of bicycling might be able to reconnect American consumers to their experiences as children while also dealing with the root causes of their feelings of intimidation—thus revealing a large untapped market.

The design team, responsible for every aspect of what was envisioned as a holistic experience, came up with the concept of "Coasting." Coasting would aim to entice lapsed bikers into an activity that was simple, straightforward, and fun. Coasting bikes, built more for pleasure than for sport, would have no controls on the handlebars, no cables snaking along the frame. As on the earliest bikes many of us rode, the brakes would be applied by backpedaling. With the help of an onboard computer, a minimalist three gears would shift automatically as the bicycle gained speed or slowed. The bikes would feature comfortably padded seats, be easy to operate, and require relatively little maintenance.

Three major manufacturers—Trek, Raleigh, and Giant—developed new bikes incorporating innovative components from Shimano. But the design team didn't stop with the bike itself. In-store retailing strategies were created for independent bike dealers, in part to alleviate the discomfort that biking novices felt in stores designed to serve enthusiasts. The team developed a brand that identified Coasting as a way to enjoy life. ("Chill. Explore. Dawdle. Lollygag. First one there's a rotten egg.") And it designed a public relations campaign—in collaboration with local governments and cycling organizations—that identified safe places to ride.

Although many others became involved in the project when it reached the implementation phase, the application of design thinking in the earliest stages of innovation is what led to this complete solution. Indeed, the single thing one would have expected the design team to be responsible for—the look of the bikes—was intentionally deferred to later in the development process, when the team created a reference design to inspire the bike companies' own design teams. After a successful launch in 2007, seven more bicycle manufacturers signed up to produce Coasting bikes in 2008.

Coasting

A **sketch** (top, seat plus helmet storage) and a **prototype** (middle) show elements of Coasting bicycles. Shimano's Coasting **website** (bottom) points users to safe bike paths.

Taking a Systems View

Many of the world's most successful brands create breakthrough ideas that are inspired by a deep understanding of consumers' lives and use the principles of design to innovate and build value. Sometimes innovation has to account for vast differences in cultural and socioeconomic conditions. In such cases design thinking can suggest creative alternatives to the assumptions made in developed societies.

India's Aravind Eye Care System is probably the world's largest provider of eye care. From April 2006 to March 2007 Aravind served more than 2.3 million patients and performed more than 270,000 surgeries. Founded in 1976 by Dr. G. Venkataswamy, Aravind has as its mission nothing less than the eradication of needless blindness among India's population, including the rural poor, through the effective delivery of superior ophthalmic care. (One of the company's slogans is "Quality is for everyone.") From 11 beds in Dr. Venkataswamy's home, Aravind has grown to encompass five hospitals (three others are under Aravind management), a plant that manufactures ophthalmic products, a research foundation, and a training center.

Aravind's execution of its mission and model is in some respects reminiscent of Edison's holistic concept of electric power delivery. The challenge the company faces is logistic: how best to deliver eye care to populations far removed from the urban centers where Aravind's hospitals are located. Aravind calls itself an "eye care system" for a reason: Its business goes beyond ophthalmic care per se to transmit expert practice to populations that have historically lacked access. The company saw its network of hospitals as a beginning rather than an end.

Much of its innovative energy has focused on bringing both preventive care and diagnostic screening to the countryside. Since 1990 Aravind has held "eye camps" in India's rural areas, in an effort to register patients, administer eye exams, teach eye care, and identify people who may require surgery or advanced diagnostic services or who have conditions that warrant monitoring.

Aravind

Aravind's outreach to rural patients frequently brings basic **diagnostic tools** (top and center) and an advanced satellite-linked **telemedicine truck** (bottom) to remote areas of India.

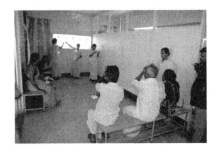

In 2006 and early 2007 Aravind eye camps screened more than 500,000 patients, of whom nearly 113,000 required surgery. Access to transportation is a common problem in rural areas, so the company provides buses that take patients needing further treatment to one of its urban facilities and then home again. Over the years it has bolstered its diagnostic capabilities in the field with telemedicine trucks, which enable doctors back at Aravind's hospitals to participate in care decisions. In recent years Aravind's analysis of its screening data has led to specialized eye camps for certain demographic groups, such as school-age children and industrial and government workers; the company also holds camps specifically to screen for eye diseases associated with diabetes. All these services are free for the roughly 60% of patients who cannot afford to pay.

In developing its system of care, Aravind has consistently exhibited many characteristics of design thinking. It has used as a creative springboard two constraints: the poverty and remoteness of its clientele and its own lack of access to expensive solutions. For example, a pair of intraocular lenses made in the West costs $200, which severely limited the number of patients Aravind could help. Rather than try to persuade suppliers to change the way they did things, Aravind built its own solution: a manufacturing plant in the basement of one of its hospitals. It eventually discovered that it could use relatively inexpensive technology to produce lenses for $4 a pair.

Throughout its history—defined by the constraints of poverty, ignorance, and an enormous unmet need—Aravind has built a systemic solution to a complex social and medical problem.

Getting Back to the Surface

I argued earlier that design thinking can lead to innovation that goes beyond aesthetics, but that doesn't mean that form and aesthetics are unimportant. Magazines like to publish photographs of the newest, coolest products for a reason: They are sexy and appeal to our emotions. Great design satisfies both our needs and our desires. Often the emotional connection to a product or an image is what engages us in the first place. Time and again we see successful products that were not necessarily the first to market but were the first to appeal to us emotionally *and* functionally. In other words, they do the job and we love them. The iPod was not the first MP3 player, but it was the first to be delightful. Target's products appeal emotionally through design and functionally through price—simultaneously.

This idea will grow ever more important in the future. As Daniel Pink writes in his book *A Whole New Mind*, "Abundance has satisfied, and even over-satisfied, the material needs of millions—boosting the significance of beauty and emotion and accelerating individuals' search for meaning." As more of our basic needs are met, we increasingly expect sophisticated experiences that are emotionally satisfying and meaningful. These experiences will not be simple products. They will be complex combinations of products, services, spaces, and information. They will be the ways we get educated, the ways we are entertained, the ways we stay healthy, the ways we share and communicate. Design thinking is a tool for imagining these experiences as well as giving them a desirable form.

One example of experiential innovation comes from a financial services company. In late 2005 Bank of America launched a new savings account service called "Keep the Change." IDEO, working with a team from the bank, helped identify a consumer behavior that many people will recognize: After paying cash for something, we put the coins we received in change into a jar at home. Once the jar is full, we take the coins to the bank and deposit them in a savings account. For many people, it's an easy way of saving. Bank of America's innovation was to build this behavior into a debit card account. Customers who use their debit cards to make purchases can now choose to have the total rounded up to the nearest dollar and the difference deposited in their savings accounts.

The success of this innovation lay in its appeal to an instinctive desire we have to put money aside in a painless and invisible way. Keep the Change creates an experience that feels natural because it models behavior that many of us already exhibit. To be sure, Bank of America sweetens the deal by matching 100% of the change saved in the first three months and 5% of annual totals (up to $250) thereafter.

How to Make Design Thinking Part of the Innovation Drill

- **Begin at the beginning.** Involve design thinkers at the very start of the innovation process, before any direction has been set. Design thinking will help you explore more ideas more quickly than you could otherwise.

- **Take a human-centered approach.** Along with business and technology considerations, innovation should factor in human behavior, needs, and preferences. Human-centered design thinking—especially when it includes research based on direct observation—will capture unexpected insights and produce innovation that more precisely reflects what consumers want.

- **Try early and often.** Create an expectation of rapid experimentation and prototyping. Encourage teams to create a prototype in the first week of a project. Measure progress with a metric such as average time to first prototype or number of consumers exposed to prototypes during the life of a program.

- **Seek outside help.** Expand the innovation ecosystem by looking for opportunities to cocreate with customers and consumers. Exploit Web 2.0 networks to enlarge the effective scale of your innovation team.

- **Blend big and small projects.** Manage a portfolio of innovation that stretches from shorter-term incremental ideas to longer-term

This encourages customers to try it out. But the real payoff is emotional: the gratification that comes with monthly statements showing customers they've saved money without even trying.

In less than a year the program attracted 2.5 million customers. It is credited with 700,000 new checking accounts and a million new savings accounts. Enrollment now totals more than 5 million people who together have saved more than $500 million. Keep the Change demonstrates that design thinking can identify an aspect of human behavior and then convert it into both a customer benefit and a business value.

Thomas Edison represents what many of us think of as a golden age of American innovation—a time when new ideas transformed every aspect of our lives. The need for transformation is, if anything, revolutionary ones. Expect business units to drive and fund incremental innovation, but be willing to initiate revolutionary innovation from the top.

- **Budget to the pace of innovation.** Design thinking happens quickly, yet the route to market can be unpredictable. Don't constrain the pace at which you can innovate by relying on cumbersome budgeting cycles. Be prepared to rethink your funding approach as projects proceed and teams learn more about opportunities.

- **Find talent any way you can.** Look to hire from interdisciplinary programs like the new Institute of Design at Stanford and progressive business schools like Rotman, in Toronto. People with more-conventional design backgrounds can push solutions far beyond your expectations. You may even be able to train nondesigners with the right attributes to excel in design-thinking roles.

- **Design for the cycle.** In many businesses people move every 12 to 18 months. But design projects may take longer than that to get from day one through implementation. Plan assignments so that design thinkers go from inspiration to ideation to implementation. Experiencing the full cycle builds better judgment and creates great long-term benefits for the organization.

greater now than ever before. No matter where we look, we see problems that can be solved only through innovation: unaffordable or unavailable health care, billions of people trying to live on just a few dollars a day, energy usage that outpaces the planet's ability to support it, education systems that fail many students, companies whose traditional markets are disrupted by new technologies or demographic shifts. These problems all have people at their heart. They require a human-centered, creative, iterative, and practical approach to finding the best ideas and ultimate solutions. Design thinking is just such an approach to innovation.

Originally published in June 2008. Reprint R0806E

Why Design Thinking Works

by Jeanne M. Liedtka

OCCASIONALLY, A NEW WAY of organizing work leads to extraordinary improvements. Total quality management did that in manufacturing in the 1980s by combining a set of tools—kanban cards, quality circles, and so on—with the insight that people on the shop floor could do much higher-level work than they usually were asked to. That blend of tools and insight, applied to a work process, can be thought of as a *social technology*.

In a recent seven-year study in which I looked in depth at 50 projects from a range of sectors, including business, health care, and social services, I have seen that another social technology, design thinking, has the potential to do for innovation exactly what TQM did for manufacturing: unleash people's full creative energies, win their commitment, and radically improve processes. By now most executives have at least heard about design thinking's tools—ethnographic research, an emphasis on reframing problems and experimentation, the use of diverse teams, and so on—if not tried them. But what people may not understand is the subtler way that design thinking gets around the human biases (for example, rootedness in the status quo) or attachments to specific behavioral norms ("That's how we do things here") that time and again block the exercise of imagination.

In this article I'll explore a variety of human tendencies that get in the way of innovation and describe how design thinking's tools and clear process steps help teams break free of them. Let's begin by looking at what organizations need from innovation—and at why their efforts to obtain it often fall short.

The Challenges of Innovation

To be successful, an innovation process must deliver three things: superior solutions, lower risks and costs of change, and employee buy-in. Over the years businesspeople have developed useful tactics for achieving those outcomes. But when trying to apply them, organizations frequently encounter new obstacles and trade-offs.

Superior solutions

Defining problems in obvious, conventional ways, not surprisingly, often leads to obvious, conventional solutions. *Asking a more interesting question* can help teams discover more-original ideas. The risk is that some teams may get indefinitely hung up exploring a problem, while action-oriented managers may be too impatient to take the time to figure out what question they should be asking.

It's also widely accepted that solutions are much better when they incorporate *user-driven criteria*. Market research can help companies understand those criteria, but the hurdle here is that it's hard for customers to know they want something that doesn't yet exist.

Finally, bringing *diverse voices* into the process is also known to improve solutions. This can be difficult to manage, however, if conversations among people with opposing views deteriorate into divisive debates.

Lower risks and costs

Uncertainty is unavoidable in innovation. That's why innovators often build a *portfolio of options*. The trade-off is that too many ideas dilute focus and resources. To manage this tension, innovators must be willing to let go of bad ideas—to "call the baby ugly," as a manager in one of my studies described it. Unfortunately, people often find it easier to kill the creative (and arguably riskier) ideas than to kill the incremental ones.

Idea in Brief

The Problem

While we know a lot about what practices stimulate new ideas and creative solutions, most innovation teams struggle to realize their benefits.

The Cause

People's intrinsic biases and behavioral habits inhibit the exercise of the imagination and protect unspoken assumptions about what will or will not work.

The Solution

Design thinking provides a structured process that helps innovators break free of counterproductive tendencies that thwart innovation. Like TQM, it is a social technology that blends practical tools with insights into human nature.

Employee buy-in

An innovation won't succeed unless a company's employees get behind it. The surest route to winning their support is to involve them in the process of generating ideas. The danger is that the involvement of many people with different perspectives will create chaos and incoherence.

Underlying the trade-offs associated with achieving these outcomes is a more fundamental tension. In a stable environment, efficiency is achieved by driving variation out of the organization. But in an unstable world, variation becomes the organization's friend, because it opens new paths to success. However, who can blame leaders who must meet quarterly targets for doubling down on efficiency, rationality, and centralized control?

To manage all the trade-offs, organizations need a social technology that addresses these behavioral obstacles as well as the counterproductive biases of human beings. And as I'll explain next, design thinking fits that bill.

The Beauty of Structure

Experienced designers often complain that design thinking is too structured and linear. And for them, that's certainly true. But managers on innovation teams generally are not designers and also aren't used to doing face-to-face research with customers, getting deeply

Shaping the innovator's journey

What makes design thinking a social technology is its ability to counteract the biases of innovators and change the way they engage in the innovation process.

Problem	Design thinking	Improved outcome
Innovators are:		
Trapped in their own expertise and experience	**Provides immersion** in the user's experience, shifting an innovator's mindset toward . . .	A better understanding of those being designed for
Overwhelmed by the volume and messiness of qualitative data	**Makes sense** of data by organizing it into themes and patterns, pointing the innovator toward . . .	New insights and possibilities
Divided by differences in team members' perspectives	**Builds alignment** as insights are translated into design criteria, moving an innovation team toward . . .	Convergence around what really matters to users
Confronted by too many disparate but familiar ideas	**Encourages the emergence** of fresh ideas through a focused inquiry, shifting team members toward . . .	A limited but diverse set of potential new solutions
Constrained by existing biases about what does or doesn't work	**Fosters articulation** of the conditions necessary to each idea's success and transitions a team toward . . .	Clarity on make-or-break assumptions that enables the design of meaningful experiments
Lacking a shared understanding of new ideas and often unable to get good feedback from users	**Offers pre-experiences** to users through very rough prototypes that help innovators get . . .	Accurate feedback at low cost and an understanding of potential solutions' true value
Afraid of change and ambiguity surrounding the new future	**Delivers learning in action** as experiments engage staff and users, helping them build . . .	A shared commitment and confidence in the new product or strategy

immersed in their perspectives, cocreating with stakeholders, and designing and executing experiments. Structure and linearity help managers try to adjust to these new behaviors.

As Kaaren Hanson, formerly the head of design innovation at Intuit and now Facebook's design product director, has explained:

"Anytime you're trying to change people's behavior, you need to start them off with a lot of structure, so they don't have to think. A lot of what we do is habit, and it's hard to change those habits, but having very clear guardrails can help us."

Organized processes keep people on track and curb the tendency to spend too long exploring a problem or to impatiently skip ahead. They also instill confidence. Most humans are driven by a fear of mistakes, so they focus more on preventing errors than on seizing opportunities. They opt for inaction rather than action when a choice risks failure. But there is no innovation without action—so psychological safety is essential. The physical props and highly formatted tools of design thinking deliver that sense of security, helping would-be innovators move more assuredly through the discovery of customer needs, idea generation, and idea testing.

In most organizations the application of design thinking involves seven activities. Each generates a clear output that the next activity converts to another output until the organization arrives at an implementable innovation. But at a deeper level, something else is happening—something that executives generally are not aware of. Though ostensibly geared to understanding and molding the experiences of customers, each design-thinking activity also reshapes the experiences of the *innovators themselves* in profound ways.

Customer Discovery

Many of the best-known methods of the design-thinking discovery process relate to identifying the "job to be done." Adapted from the fields of ethnography and sociology, these methods concentrate on examining what makes for a meaningful customer journey rather than on the collection and analysis of data. This exploration entails three sets of activities:

Immersion

Traditionally, customer research has been an impersonal exercise. An expert, who may well have preexisting theories about customer preferences, reviews feedback from focus groups, surveys, and, if available, data on current behavior, and draws inferences about needs. The better the data, the better the inferences. The trouble is, this grounds people in the already articulated needs that the data reflects. They see the data through the lens of their own biases. And they don't recognize needs people have *not* expressed.

Design thinking takes a different approach: Identify hidden needs by having the innovator live the customer's experience. Consider what happened at the Kingwood Trust, a UK charity helping adults with autism and Asperger's syndrome. One design team member, Katie Gaudion, got to know Pete, a nonverbal adult with autism. The first time she observed him at his home, she saw him engaged in seemingly damaging acts—like picking at a leather sofa and rubbing indents in a wall. She started by documenting Pete's behavior and defined the problem as how to prevent such destructiveness.

But on her second visit to Pete's home, she asked herself: What if Pete's actions were motivated by something other than a destructive impulse? Putting her personal perspective aside, she mirrored his behavior and discovered how satisfying his activities actually felt. "Instead of a ruined sofa, I now perceived Pete's sofa as an object wrapped in fabric that is fun to pick," she explained. "Pressing my ear against the wall and feeling the vibrations of the music above, I felt a slight tickle in my ear whilst rubbing the smooth and beautiful indentation . . . So instead of a damaged wall, I perceived it as a pleasant and relaxing audio-tactile experience."

Katie's immersion in Pete's world not only produced a deeper understanding of his challenges but called into question an unexamined bias about the residents, who had been perceived as disability sufferers that needed to be kept safe. Her experience caused her to ask herself another new question: Instead of designing just for residents' disabilities and safety, how could the innovation team design for their strengths and pleasures? That led to the creation of living spaces, gardens, and new activities aimed at enabling people with autism to live fuller and more pleasurable lives.

Sense making

Immersion in user experiences provides raw material for deeper insights. But finding patterns and making sense of the mass of qualitative data collected is a daunting challenge. Time and again, I have seen initial enthusiasm about the results of ethnographic tools fade as nondesigners become overwhelmed by the volume of information and the messiness of searching for deeper insights. It is here that the structure of design thinking really comes into its own.

One of the most effective ways to make sense of the knowledge generated by immersion is a design-thinking exercise called the Gallery Walk. In it the core innovation team selects the most important data gathered during the discovery process and writes it down on large posters. Often these posters showcase individuals who have been interviewed, complete with their photos and quotations capturing their perspectives. The posters are hung around a room, and key stakeholders are invited to tour this gallery and write down on Post-it notes the bits of data they consider essential to new designs. The stakeholders then form small teams, and in a carefully orchestrated process, their Post-it observations are shared, combined, and sorted by theme into clusters that the group mines for insights. This process overcomes the danger that innovators will be unduly influenced by their own biases and see only what they want to see, because it makes the people who were interviewed feel vivid and real to those browsing the gallery. It creates a common database and facilitates collaborators' ability to interact, reach shared insights together, and challenge one another's individual takeaways—another critical guard against biased interpretations.

Alignment

The final stage in the discovery process is a series of workshops and seminar discussions that ask in some form the question, If anything were possible, what job would the design do well? The focus on possibilities, rather than on the constraints imposed by the status quo, helps diverse teams have more-collaborative and creative discussions about the design criteria, or the set of key features that an ideal innovation should have. Establishing a spirit of inquiry deepens dissatisfaction with the status quo and makes it easier for teams to reach consensus throughout the innovation process. And down the road, when the portfolio of ideas is winnowed, agreement on the design criteria will give novel ideas a fighting chance against safer incremental ones.

Consider what happened at Monash Health, an integrated hospital and health care system in Melbourne, Australia. Mental health clinicians there had long been concerned about the frequency of patient relapses—usually in the form of drug overdoses and suicide attempts—but consensus on how to address this problem eluded them. In an effort to get to the bottom of it, clinicians traced the experiences of specific patients through the treatment process. One patient, Tom, emerged as emblematic in their study. His experience included three face-to-face visits with different clinicians, 70 touchpoints, 13 different case managers, and 18 handoffs during the interval between his initial visit and his relapse.

The team members held a series of workshops in which they asked clinicians this question: Did Tom's current care exemplify why they had entered health care? As people discussed their motivations for becoming doctors and nurses, they came to realize that improving Tom's outcome might depend as much on their sense of duty to Tom himself as it did on their clinical activity. Everyone bought into this conclusion, which made designing a new treatment process—centered on the patient's needs rather than perceived best practices—proceed smoothly and successfully. After its implementation, patient-relapse rates fell by 60%.

Idea Generation

Once they understand customers' needs, innovators move on to identify and winnow down specific solutions that conform to the criteria they've identified.

Emergence

The first step here is to set up a dialogue about potential solutions, carefully planning who will participate, what challenge they will be given, and how the conversation will be structured. After using the design criteria to do some individual brainstorming, participants gather to share ideas and build on them creatively—as opposed to simply negotiating compromises when differences arise.

When Children's Health System of Texas, the sixth-largest pediatric medical center in the United States, identified the need for a new strategy, the organization, led by the vice president of population health, Peter Roberts, applied design thinking to reimagine its business model. During the discovery process, clinicians set aside their bias that what mattered most was medical intervention. They came to understand that intervention alone wouldn't work if the local population in Dallas didn't have the time or ability to seek out medical knowledge and didn't have strong support networks—something few families in the area enjoyed. The clinicians also realized that the medical center couldn't successfully address problems on its own; the community would need to be central to any solution. So Children's Health invited its community partners to codesign a new wellness ecosystem whose boundaries (and resources) would stretch far beyond the medical center. Deciding to start small and tackle a single condition, the team gathered to create a new model for managing asthma.

The session brought together hospital administrators, physicians, nurses, social workers, parents of patients, and staff from Dallas's school districts, housing authority, YMCA, and faith-based organizations. First, the core innovation team shared learning from the discovery process. Next, each attendee thought independently about the capabilities that his or her institution might contribute toward addressing the children's problems, jotting down ideas on sticky notes. Then each attendee was invited to join a small group at one of five tables, where the participants shared individual ideas, grouped them into common themes, and envisioned what an ideal experience would look like for the young patients and their families.

Champions of change usually emerge from these kinds of conversations, which greatly improves the chances of successful implementation. (All too often, good ideas die on the vine in the absence of people with a personal commitment to making them happen.) At Children's Health, the partners invited into the project galvanized the community to act and forged and maintained the relationships in their institutions required to realize the new vision. Housing authority representatives drove changes in housing codes, charging inspectors with incorporating children's health issues (like the presence of mold) into their assessments. Local pediatricians adopted a set of standard asthma protocols, and parents of children with asthma took on a significant role as peer counselors providing intensive education to other families through home visits.

Articulation

Typically, emergence activities generate a number of competing ideas, more or less attractive and more or less feasible. In the next step, articulation, innovators surface and question their implicit assumptions. Managers are often bad at this, because of many behavioral biases, such as overoptimism, confirmation bias, and fixation on first solutions. When assumptions aren't challenged, discussions around what will or won't work become deadlocked, with each person advocating from his or her own understanding of how the world works.

In contrast, design thinking frames the discussion as an inquiry into what would have to be true about the world for an idea to be feasible. (See "Management Is Much More Than a Science," by Roger L. Martin and Tony Golsby-Smith, HBR, September–October 2017.) An example of this comes from the Ignite Accelerator program of the U.S. Department of Health and Human Services. At the Whiteriver Indian reservation hospital in Arizona, a team led by Marliza Rivera, a young quality control officer, sought to reduce wait times in the hospital's emergency room, which were sometimes as long as six hours.

The team's initial concept, borrowed from Johns Hopkins Hospital in Baltimore, was to install an electronic kiosk for check-in. As team members began to apply design thinking, however, they were asked to surface their assumptions about why the idea would work. It was only then that they realized that their patients, many of whom were elderly Apache speakers, were unlikely to be comfortable with computer technology. Approaches that worked in urban Baltimore would not work in Whiteriver, so this idea could be safely set aside.

At the end of the idea generation process, innovators will have a portfolio of well-thought-through, though possibly quite different, ideas. The assumptions underlying them will have been carefully vetted, and the conditions necessary for their success will be achievable. The ideas will also have the support of committed teams, who will be prepared to take on the responsibility of bringing them to market.

The Testing Experience

Companies often regard prototyping as a process of fine-tuning a product or service that has already largely been developed. But in design thinking, prototyping is carried out on far-from-finished products. It's about users' iterative experiences with a work in progress. This means that quite radical changes—including complete redesigns—can occur along the way.

Pre-experience

Neuroscience research indicates that helping people "pre-experience" something novel—or to put it another way, *imagine* it incredibly vividly—results in more-accurate assessments of the novelty's value. That's why design thinking calls for the creation of basic, low-cost artifacts that will capture the essential features of the proposed user experience. These are not literal prototypes—and they are often much rougher than the "minimum viable products" that lean startups test with customers. But what these artifacts lose in fidelity, they gain in flexibility, because they can easily be altered in response to what's learned by exposing users to them. And their incompleteness invites interaction.

Such artifacts can take many forms. The layout of a new medical office building at Kaiser Permanente, for example, was tested by hanging bedsheets from the ceiling to mark future walls. Nurses and physicians were invited to interact with staffers who were playing the role of patients and to suggest how spaces could be adjusted to better facilitate treatment. At Monash Health, a program called Monash Watch—aimed at using telemedicine to keep vulnerable populations healthy at home and reduce their hospitalization rates—used detailed storyboards to help hospital administrators and government policy makers envision this new approach in practice, without building a digital prototype.

Learning in action

Real-world experiments are an essential way to assess new ideas and identify the changes needed to make them workable. But such tests offer another, less obvious kind of value: They help reduce employees' and customers' quite normal fear of change.

Consider an idea proposed by Don Campbell, a professor of medicine, and Keith Stockman, a manager of operations research at Monash Health. As part of Monash Watch, they suggested hiring laypeople to be "telecare" guides who would act as "professional neighbors," keeping in frequent telephone contact with patients at high risk of multiple hospital admissions. Campbell and Stockman hypothesized that lower-wage laypeople who were carefully selected, trained in health literacy and empathy skills, and backed by a decision support system and professional coaches they could involve as needed could help keep the at-risk patients healthy at home.

Their proposal was met with skepticism. Many of their colleagues held a strong bias against letting anyone besides a health professional perform such a service for patients with complex issues, but using health professionals in the role would have been unaffordable. Rather than debating this point, however, the innovation team members acknowledged the concerns and engaged their colleagues in the codesign of an experiment testing that assumption. Three hundred patients later, the results were in: Overwhelmingly positive patient feedback and a demonstrated reduction in bed use and emergency room visits, corroborated by independent consultants, quelled the fears of the skeptics.

As we have seen, the structure of design thinking creates a natural flow from research to rollout. Immersion in the customer experience produces data, which is transformed into insights, which help teams agree on design criteria they use to brainstorm solutions. Assumptions about what's critical to the success of those solutions are examined and then tested with rough prototypes that help teams further develop innovations and prepare them for real-world experiments. Along the way, design-thinking processes counteract human biases that thwart creativity while addressing the challenges typically faced in reaching superior solutions, lowered costs and risks, and employee buy-in. Recognizing organizations as collections of human beings who are motivated by varying perspectives and emotions, design thinking emphasizes engagement, dialogue, and learning. By involving customers and other stakeholders in the definition of the problem and the development of solutions, design thinking garners a broad commitment to change. And by supplying a structure to the innovation process, design thinking helps innovators collaborate and agree on what is essential to the outcome at every phase. It does this not only by overcoming workplace politics but by shaping the experiences of the innovators, and of their key stakeholders and implementers, at every step. *That* is social technology at work.

Originally published in September–October 2018. Reprint R1805D

The Right Way to Lead Design Thinking

by Christian Bason and Robert D. Austin

ANNE LIND, THE HEAD of the national agency in Denmark that evaluates the insurance claims of injured workers and decides on their compensation, had a crisis on her hands. Oddly, it emerged from a project that had seemed to be on a path to success. The project employed design thinking in an effort to improve the services delivered by her organization. The members of her project team immersed themselves in the experiences of clients, establishing rapport and empathizing with them in a bid to see the world through their eyes. The team interviewed and unobtrusively video-recorded clients as they described their situations and their experiences with the agency's case management. The approach led to a surprising revelation: The agency's processes were designed largely to serve its own wants and needs (to be efficient and to make claims assessment easy for the staff) rather than those of clients, who typically had gone through a traumatic event and were trying to return to a productive normal life.

The feedback was eye-opening and launched a major transformation, Lind told us. But it was also upsetting. Poignantly captured in some of the videos was the fact that many clients felt harmed by the agency's actions. One person half-joked that he would need to be fully healthy to endure the stress of interacting with the agency. (The design team was dismayed to discover that during the claims process, clients received an average of 23 letters from the agency and others, such as hospitals and employers.) Lind's staffers had won productivity awards for the efficiency of their case-management processes and thought of themselves as competent professionals. They were shocked to hear such things from clients.

Lind decided to share the interview videos with employees across the organization, because their expertise and buy-in would be needed to develop solutions. They, too, were shocked and dismayed. Lind worried that many of them were taking it too hard. She wanted them to be motivated, not disabled. It was a moment that called for leadership. Her organization looked to her to help it process this troubling information and figure out what to do. What she did next would determine whether people rose to the challenge of transforming how they helped clients or sank into demoralized frustration.

Even more than other change-management processes, design thinking requires active and effective leadership to keep efforts on a path to success. Much has been written, in HBR and elsewhere, about how organizations can use design thinking for innovation (see "Design Thinking," HBR, June 2008, and "Design Thinking Comes of Age," HBR, September 2015). Our in-depth study of almost two dozen major projects within large private- and public-sector organizations in five countries suggests that effective leadership is critical to success. We focused not on how individual design-thinking teams did their work but on how the senior executives who commissioned the work interacted with and enabled it.

Typically, leaders sponsored project teams—composed of external consultants or in-house specialized units—that worked with a subset of employees to generate solutions that were eventually implemented more widely, often across the entire organization. In some cases, when change would involve different areas of an organization and the core team lacked expertise in their processes, the project expanded to include people in those areas—an approach that also helped secure their buy-in. In most cases the leaders who commissioned these projects had no prior experience with design thinking. Although some were involved more directly than others, all were looking to the approach to help them achieve their strategic objectives.

Idea in Brief

The Challenge

Design-thinking methods—such as empathizing with users and conducting experiments knowing many will fail—often seem subjective and personal to employees accustomed to being told to be rational and objective.

The Fallout

Employees can be shocked and dismayed by findings, feel like they are spinning their wheels, or

find it difficult to shed preconceptions about the product or service they've been providing. Their anxieties may derail the project.

The Remedy

Leaders—without being heavy-handed—need to help teams make the space and time for new ideas to emerge and maintain an overall sense of direction and purpose.

Why Strong Leadership Is Crucial

"Design thinking" can mean different things, but it usually describes processes, methods, and tools for creating human-centered products, services, solutions, and experiences. It involves establishing a personal connection with the users.

But to employees long accustomed to being told to be rational and objective, such methods can seem subjective and overly personal. Of course, businesses want to understand their customers—but design-thinking connections with customers can feel uncomfortably emotive and sometimes overwhelmingly affecting.

The challenges don't end there. Another potentially unsettling aspect of design-thinking methods is their reliance on divergent thinking. They ask employees to not race to the finish line or converge on an answer as quickly as possible but to expand the number of options—to go sideways for a while rather than forward. That can be difficult for people accustomed to valuing a clear direction, cost savings, efficiency, and so on. It can feel like "spinning wheels"—which in a way it is.

As if that were not enough, design-thinking approaches call on employees to repeatedly experience something they have historically tried to avoid: failure. The iterative prototyping and testing involved in these methods work best when they produce lots of negative results—outcomes that show what *doesn't* work. But piling up seemingly unsuccessful outcomes is uncomfortable for most people.

Enduring the discomfort of design thinking is worth it, because great new possibilities for change, improvement, and innovation can result. The truth is that the same aspects of design-thinking methods that make them difficult for employees to handle are also the source of their power.

Consequently, employees who are unfamiliar with design thinking (usually the majority) need the guidance and support of leaders to navigate the unfamiliar landscape and productively channel their reactions to the approach. Our research has identified three categories of practice that executives can use to lead design-thinking projects to success: leveraging empathy, encouraging divergence and navigating ambiguity, and rehearsing new futures.

Leveraging Empathy

In the early phases of a design-thinking process, employees working on a project need to set aside their preconceptions about the product or service they are offering. Leaders can help them do this by endorsing the process, which uses information about customers to evoke empathy in employees and get them to question how their actions affect customers. Our research shows, however, that leaders must do more than back the process. They also need to support employees who are dealing with distressing emotions that arise when the effectiveness of their work is questioned. Unexpected findings can generate defensiveness and fear, interfering with empathy and undermining motivation.

Lind understood that she had to turn the revelation about clients' experiences with her agency from a morale buster into a positive force for change. That meant getting employees to focus on customers rather than themselves. She accomplished that by involving people across the organization in interpreting findings from the early stages of the design-thinking project and then assigning mid-level managers to orchestrate idea-generation exercises in their units. One group came up with the notion of making the case-management process easier for clients to navigate by posting a visualization of it on the agency's website. Another group suggested a "Got Questions?" hotline on which clients could easily obtain help. In effect, Lind motivated people to think in terms of steps that individually might not solve the whole problem or be a final solution but would move things in the right direction.

Consider also a design-thinking project led by Mette Rosendal Darmer, the head nurse at Denmark's National Hospital. Interviews conducted by her project team suggested that patients felt confused, worried, fearful, and sometimes humiliated while going through the hospital's heart clinic processes. Darmer shared the feedback with the nearly 40 doctors, nurses, and administrative staffers who played major roles in the clinic's work. Those employees, whose help Darmer knew she would need to develop ideas for addressing patients' concerns, were taken aback: They thought of themselves as delivering services that restored patients to healthy lives. Darmer intended the effect: "What I wanted was to disturb them," she told us. But she did not stop at surfacing the disconnect; she also suggested practical ways of framing the new realizations to make them a powerful impetus for organizational and process change.

The reframing that ultimately proved most useful called on staff members to ask themselves, "What if the patient's time were viewed as more important than the doctor's?" This shift in perspective led to the achievable goal of optimizing the patient's journey, which guided the eventual process redesign. But Darmer had to actively legitimize the shift; her staffers were concerned that ceasing to optimize efficiency would be unwelcome, because it might increase costs. She assured them that the clinic supported the goal of putting patients first. And in the end, costs didn't rise, because improving the patient experience led to a 50% reduction in overnight stays.

The takeaway from both cases: Leaders need to push employees to open up but then be supportive about how they feel afterward—to help them get on a positive path and not brood or act defensive when confronted with deficiencies in existing practices. They need to frame the findings as opportunities for redesign and improvement rather than as performance problems.

The leaders we studied worked hard to illuminate users' real needs, even if the process initially struck employees as pointless or the findings made them uncomfortable. Poula Sangill, the leader of an organization that delivers prepared meals to senior citizens in the municipality of Holstebro, Denmark, was somewhat atypical of the leaders in our study, because she took a direct role in leading the design-thinking process. When she first proposed an improvement project, the appointed team of mid-level managers became extremely defensive and resistant to the notion that change was possible: They complained about how little time was allocated for food services (10 minutes per delivery) and insisted that nothing could be done in such a short time. In response, Sangill ran them through a step-by-step role play of the process to look for opportunities to improve even within the time constraints. Eventually her team began to offer ideas.

The leaders we studied also pushed their employees to go beyond their accustomed reliance on statistics to get close to what users were experiencing and how they felt about it. Employees were rarely familiar with the ethnographic methods used in design thinking. Leaders had to de-emphasize traditional consulting studies and instead arrange circumstances—guided by design-thinking experts—that put employees into user situations. For example, when the New York City Department of Housing Preservation and Development was working on new offerings, leaders arranged for employees to spend weeks in the field interacting with people who lived in rent-controlled properties in Manhattan. The goal was to help them understand renters' daily lives. Through observational studies and interviews employees could identify and experience firsthand the services that really mattered to residents and how offerings might be reconceived.

Leaders encouraged project teams to gather and later present their data to other employees in evocative formats, such as audio recordings or videos of people in their own contexts, rather than in the dry tables and graphs commonly used in the past. Gathering information in such forms achieves several purposes: It ensures that employees gain a deep understanding of users' circumstances. It provides a way of communicating those circumstances powerfully to others. And, if well handled by the leader, it delivers an emotional payload to motivate and generate change. To remember why change is needed, one has only to go back and listen to the voices in the recordings.

Encouraging Divergence and Navigating Ambiguity

The exemplary leaders we observed ensured that their design-thinking project teams made the space and time for diverse new ideas to emerge and also maintained an overall sense of direction and purpose. It's up to leaders to help their people resist the urge to converge quickly on a solution without feeling they lack direction.

The deputy dean of Stenhus High School, in Holbaek, Denmark, asked a team of nine teachers to come up with suggestions for transforming a program. After they set to work, the dean deliberately broke from her usual practice of closely scrutinizing progress, frequently requesting updates, and pressuring the team to complete the project quickly. Team members reported being baffled when expected management interventions failed to occur and they were repeatedly sent back to come up with more ideas. "You really didn't try to control us," they noted after a sustained period of fruitful ideation. "No, I really didn't," the dean told us. "It was a loss of control, but it was a positive loss of control."

Peter Gadsdon, the head of customer insight and service design for the London borough of Lewisham, arranged to video-record frontline workers' interactions with citizens in the homelessness services unit. This was not normal practice—and citizens' privacy had to be protected. But once it was approved and arranged by Gadsdon, these videos could be used, in accordance with common design-thinking practice, to spark ideas. "The staff interviewed many different people over a period of about three weeks, and just caught lots and lots of footage," Gadsdon told us. One clip showed children of non-English-speaking immigrants translating their parents' conversation with caseworkers. This was counter to the preferred practice of using a professional translator to avoid traumatizing young children by involving them in conversations about complex adult issues such as potential homelessness. After viewing the clip, Gadsdon asked frontline employees, "What might we do to address this kind of problem?" The designers used the films to open up people's minds, he said, adding, "They had lots of ideas."

At Boeing we saw Larry Loftis, then a manufacturing executive at the aerospace giant, insist that process-improvement teams use an approach called the seven ways—identifying at least seven options when brainstorming possible solutions. "The first two or three come very easily," Loftis said, "but then it becomes very difficult to come up with those other solutions. You have to unanchor [from your initial thoughts] and open up your mind."

The aim of divergent thinking is to get beyond easy answers and find options that might be truly innovative. Extreme options are rarely chosen, but they can be stepping-stones to more-practical solutions. "You can get really crazy on some of them, where you know there's no way they're going to happen," Loftis told us. "But then some dialogue takes place around what if you take that idea over to the side a little bit and come up with some new idea that does work."

"Going sideways" for the purpose of generating more ideas than will ever be used and getting to ideas so crazy that they'll never fly makes some people uncomfortable. To goal-oriented people, divergent thinking can seem to generate unnecessary ambiguity about where a project is heading. Leaders need to help those people deal with their insecurities and worries.

That's not always easy, because managers may be experiencing the same feelings. "How do you explain to your staff that you are deploying a methodology you don't fully understand yourself?" a manager who ran business-support services for the city of Helsinki asked us. She had commissioned a design-thinking project to find ways to cut red tape for businesses. The main focus was streamlining the permitting process for outdoor restaurants and entertainment venues, which at the time involved as many as 14 city agencies. She answered her own question by leading by example: She shared her feelings of uncertainty with employees even as she jumped fearlessly into the process, and she communicated clearly that she saw the open-endedness of the new approach as a way of stretching for solutions, not as a lack of direction.

Rehearsing New Futures

A fundamental element of design thinking is testing possible solutions with end users, staffers, and other stakeholders in quick-and-dirty ways. Boeing calls this *try storming*—it's like brainstorming, but it goes beyond thinking up ideas to actually carrying them out in some fashion. It might entail building models or making videos of imagined future arrangements. Such tangible artifacts generate conversations that tend to be much more detailed, concrete, and useful than hypothetical discussions are. Leaders should enable this practice by providing time and resources and address skepticism about the value of the work by conveying to employees that "failed" prototypes represent progress. They should clearly spell out what they're trying to achieve and for whom they are trying to achieve it.

Seth Schoenfeld, the founding principal of Olympus Academy, a public high school in Brooklyn, New York, wanted his organization to rethink how it created learning outcomes (for example, how it taught new skills to students). His usual approach was to convene a group of teachers and students to come up with new ideas on the basis of their own experiences. In this instance he was invited to try design thinking as part of an initiative by the New York City Department of Education, which provided advisers and tools, including a video camera. Schoenfeld proposed that the team make a short video depicting a day in the life of an imaginary student in a fully digital and student-centric learning environment. People involved in the project used the video to illustrate new scenarios: teaching materials available online, lessons tailored to each student's abilities and pace of learning, follow-on courses to be instantly available upon completion of previous ones, and so on. The video, in which a student on the team played the main role, provoked rich discussions about the merits of alternative futures for the school. As they talked about the video, the principal and the teaching staff moved closer to understanding how to enact broader, visionary objectives, most of which were later realized. Since this was vastly different from their usual way of working, it helped enormously to have support and guidance come from the top.

During her project to redesign the municipal "meals on wheels" service in Holstebro, Poula Sangill asked the design-thinking team to craft a restaurant-style service, which it tested and iteratively developed with actual customers. She also asked the team members to playact various scenarios. At first employees considered the exercise silly. Eventually, though, they found that customer feedback led to ideas that they would not have come up with otherwise. Some of these, such as smaller meals to match smaller appetites, reduced costs, in keeping with an overall objective of the transformation.

Rehearsing the future requires that leaders be specific about what overarching outcomes need to be achieved. In a project aimed at transforming the customer experience, the Norwegian insurance giant Gjensidige prototyped a wide variety of ideas to arrive at three key elements of great customer service: Be friendly and empathetic; solve the customer's problem immediately; and always give customers one piece of advice they didn't expect. Although these principles may sound straightforward, they were close to revolutionary for a financial organization that had traditionally focused on risk management and control. They entailed a shift from viewing customer claims with some skepticism to systematically creating positive customer experiences. Leaders had to communicate to employees that it was OK to make that shift. To be credible, they had to react carefully if a risk was realized—for example, an employee was duped by a false claim—and signal clearly that customer service remained preeminent even when things went wrong. The transformation helped propel Gjensidige to the top in customer service and loyalty rankings among the nearly 100 companies operating in its market (Norway, Denmark, Sweden, and the Baltic states).

In testing solutions, the leaders we studied encouraged a focus on creating value not just for external clients but also for employees (and sometimes other constituencies). This broadened the potential benefits of change and secured the buy-in of multiple groups, producing longer-lasting change.

When the industrial giant Grundfos, a world leader in water-pump technology, began working on a next-generation pump, the design team knew that the control and user interface had to be highly digital. But what would that mean in practice? The natural inclination of the team was to research digital technologies and inquire into customer needs—both essential to the project, of course. But executives insisted that team members think more broadly about the constituencies for whom value would be produced—including the technicians, some of whom might work for other companies, who would be installing the pumps. What was their work context? What were their needs?

Leaders can't simply commission design-thinking projects and then step back. They must keep a watchful eye on them and be vigilant in recognizing moments when they need to engage with the team. They must help team members deal with the emotions and discomfort that are inevitable in such endeavors. They must encourage the team to take those all-important exploratory detours while also helping maintain confidence that the initiative is moving forward. At the same time, they must not be too heavy-handed: Teams need to make their own discoveries and realize that they are engaging in a creative process, not just executing management's instructions.

Leaders who commission design-thinking projects must be coaches who inspire their teams to achieve success, hand-holding when necessary but drawing back when a team hits its stride. This role isn't easy. Design thinking is challenging because it involves something more fundamental than just managing change: It involves discovering what kind of change is needed. The managers we studied demonstrated that many leaders can do it. But it takes a deep understanding of the job and an appreciation of the differences between design thinking and other approaches for bringing about organizational transformation.

Originally published in March–April 2019. Reprint R1902F

Design for Action

by Tim Brown and Roger L. Martin

THROUGHOUT MOST OF HISTORY, design was a process applied to physical objects. Raymond Loewy designed trains. Frank Lloyd Wright designed houses. Charles Eames designed furniture. Coco Chanel designed haute couture. Paul Rand designed logos.

David Kelley designed products, including (most famously) the mouse for the Apple computer.

But as it became clear that smart, effective design was behind the success of many commercial goods, companies began employing it in more and more contexts. High-tech firms that hired designers to work on hardware (to, say, come up with the shape and layout of a smartphone) began asking them to create the look and feel of user-interface software. Then designers were asked to help improve user experiences. Soon firms were treating corporate strategy making as an exercise in design. Today design is even applied to helping multiple stakeholders and organizations work better as a system.

This is the classic path of intellectual progress. Each design process is more complicated and sophisticated than the one before it. Each was enabled by learning from the preceding stage. Designers could easily turn their minds to graphical user interfaces for software because they had experience designing the hardware on which the applications would run. Having crafted better experiences for computer users, designers could readily take on nondigital experiences, like patients' hospital visits. And once they learned how to redesign the user experience in a single organization, they were more prepared to tackle the holistic experience in a system of organizations. The San

Francisco Unified School District, for example, recently worked with IDEO to help redesign the cafeteria experience across all its schools.

As design has moved further from the world of products, its tools have been adapted and extended into a distinct new discipline: design thinking. Arguably, Nobel laureate Herbert Simon got the ball rolling with the 1969 classic *The Sciences of the Artificial*, which characterized design not so much as a physical process as a way of thinking. And Richard Buchanan made a seminal advance in his 1992 article "Wicked Problems in Design Thinking," in which he proposed using design to solve extraordinarily persistent and difficult challenges.

But as the complexity of the design process increases, a new hurdle arises: the acceptance of what we might call "the designed artifact"—whether product, user experience, strategy, or complex system—by stakeholders. In the following pages we'll explain this new challenge and demonstrate how design thinking can help strategic and system innovators make the new worlds they've imagined come to pass. In fact, we'd argue that with very complex artifacts, the design of their "intervention"—their introduction and integration into the status quo—is even more critical to success than the design of the artifacts themselves.

The New Challenge

The launch of a new product that resembles a company's other offerings—say, a hybrid version of an existing car model—is typically seen as a positive thing. It produces new revenue and few perceived downsides for the organization. The new vehicle doesn't cause any meaningful changes to the organization or the way its people work, so the design isn't inherently threatening to anyone's job or to the current power structure.

Of course, introducing something new is always worrisome. The hybrid might fail in the marketplace. That would be costly and embarrassing. It might cause other vehicles in the portfolio to be phased out, producing angst for those who support the older models. Yet the designer usually pays little attention to such concerns.

Idea in Brief

The Problem

Complex new designs of products (say, an electric vehicle) or systems (like a school system) typically struggle to gain acceptance. Many good groundbreaking ideas fail in the starting gate.

Why It Happens

New products and systems often require people to change established business models and behaviors. As a result they encounter stiff resistance from their intended beneficiaries and from the people who have to deliver or operate them.

The Solution

Treat the introduction of the new product or system—the "designed artifact"—as a design challenge itself. When Intercorp Group in Peru took that approach, it won acceptance for a new technology-enabled school concept in which the teacher facilitates learning rather than serves as the sole lesson provider.

Her job is to create a truly great new car, and the knock-on effects are left to others—people in marketing or HR—to manage.

The more complex and less tangible the designed artifact is, though, the less feasible it is for the designer to ignore its potential ripple effects. The business model itself may even need to be changed. That means the introduction of the new artifact requires design attention as well.

Consider this example: A couple of years ago, MassMutual was trying to find innovative ways to persuade people younger than 40 to buy life insurance—a notoriously hard sell. The standard approach would have been to design a special life insurance product and market it in the conventional way. But MassMutual concluded that this was unlikely to work. Instead the company worked with IDEO to design a completely new type of customer experience focused more broadly on educating people about long-term financial planning.

Launched in October 2014, "Society of Grownups" was conceived as a "master's program for adulthood." Rather than delivering it purely as an online course, the company made it a multichannel experience, with state-of-the-art digital budgeting and financial-planning tools, offices with classrooms and a library customers could visit, and a curriculum that included everything from investing in a 401(k) to buying good-value wine. That approach was hugely disruptive to the organization's norms and processes, as it required not only a new brand and new digital tools but also new ways of working. In fact, every aspect of the organization had to be redesigned for the new service, which is intended to evolve as participants provide MassMutual with fresh insights into their needs.

When it comes to very complex artifacts—say, an entire business ecosystem—the problems of integrating a new design loom larger still. For example, the successful rollout of self-driving vehicles will require automobile manufacturers, technology providers, regulators, city and national governments, service firms, and end users to collaborate in new ways and engage in new behaviors. How will insurers work with manufacturers and users to analyze risk? How will data collected from self-driving cars be shared to manage traffic flows while protecting privacy?

New designs on this scale are intimidating. No wonder many genuinely innovative strategies and systems end up on a shelf somewhere—never acted on in any way. However, if you approach a large-scale change as two simultaneous and parallel challenges—the design of the artifact in question and the design of the intervention that brings it to life—you can increase the chances that it will take hold.

Designing the Intervention

Intervention design grew organically out of the iterative prototyping that was introduced to the design process as a way to better understand and predict customers' reactions to a new artifact. In the traditional approach, product developers began by studying the user and creating a product brief. Then they worked hard to create a fabulous design, which the firm launched in the market. In the design-oriented approach popularized by IDEO, the work to understand users was deeper and more ethnographic than quantitative and statistical.

Initially, that was the significant distinction between the old and new approaches. But IDEO realized that no matter how deep the up-front understanding was, designers wouldn't really be able to predict users' reactions to the final product. So IDEO's designers began to reengage with the users sooner, going to them with a very low-resolution prototype to get early feedback. Then they kept repeating the process in short cycles, steadily improving the product until the user was delighted with it. When IDEO's client actually launched the product, it was an almost guaranteed success—a phenomenon that helped make rapid prototyping a best practice.

Iterative rapid-cycle prototyping didn't just improve the artifact. It turned out to be a highly effective way to obtain the funding and organizational commitment to bring the new artifact to market. A new product, especially a relatively revolutionary one, always involves a consequential bet by the management team giving it the green light.

Often, fear of the unknown kills the new idea. With rapid prototyping, however, a team can be more confident of market success. This effect turns out to be even more important with complex, intangible designs.

In corporate strategy making, for example, a traditional approach is to have the strategist—whether in-house or a consultant—define the problem, devise the solution, and present it to the executive in charge. Often that executive has one of the following reactions: (1) This doesn't address the problems I think are critical. (2) These aren't the possibilities I would have considered. (3) These aren't the things I would have studied. (4) This isn't an answer that's compelling to me. As a consequence, winning commitment to the strategy tends to be the exception rather than the rule, especially when the strategy represents a meaningful deviation from the status quo.

The answer is iterative interaction with the decision maker. This means going to the responsible executive early on and saying, "We think this is the problem we need to solve; to what extent does that match your view?" Soon thereafter the strategy designers go back again and say, "Here are the possibilities we want to explore, given the problem definition we agreed on; to what extent are they the possibilities you imagine? Are we missing some, and are any we're considering nonstarters for you?" Later the designers return one more time to say, "We plan to do these analyses on the possibilities

The Launch Is Just One Step
in the Process

IN HIS BOOK *Sketching User Experiences*, user interface pioneer Bill Buxton describes the Apple iPod as the "overnight success" that took three years to happen. He documents the many design changes to the device that took place after its launch—and were essential to its eventual success.

As this story illustrates, a sophisticated designer recognizes that the task is first to build user acceptance of a new platform and later to add new features. When Jeff Hawkins developed the PalmPilot, the world's first successful personal digital assistant, he insisted that it focus on only three things—a calendar, contacts, and notes—because he felt users initially could not handle complexity greater than that. Over time the PalmPilot evolved to include many more functions, but by then the core market understood the experience. The initial pitch for the iPod was an extremely simple "1,000 songs in your pocket." The iTunes store, photos, games, and apps came along later, as users adopted the platform and welcomed more complexity.

As strategies and large systems become the focus of design thinking, imagining the launch as just one of many steps in introducing a new concept will become even more important. Before the launch, designers will confront increasing complexity in early dialogues with both the artifact's intended users and the decision maker responsible for the design effort. A solution with purposely lower complexity will be introduced, but it will be designed to evolve as users respond. Iteration and an explicit role for users will be a key part of any intervention design.

New information and computing technologies will make it far easier to create and share early prototypes, even if they are complex systems, and gain feedback from a more diverse population of users. In this new world, the launch of a new design ceases to be the focus. Rather, it is just one step somewhere in the middle of a carefully designed intervention.

—Tim Brown

that we've agreed are worth exploring; to what extent are they analyses that you would want done, and are we missing any?"

With this approach, the final step of actually introducing a new strategy is almost a formality. The executive responsible for greenlighting it has helped define the problem, confirm the possibilities, and affirm the analyses. The proposed direction is no longer a jolt from left field. It has gradually won commitment throughout the process of its creation.

When the challenge is introducing change to a system—by, say, establishing a new kind of business or a new kind of school—the interactions have to extend even further, to all the principal stakeholders. We'll now look at an example of this kind of intervention design, which involved a major experiment in social engineering that's taking place in Peru.

Designing a New Peru

Intercorp Group is one of Peru's biggest corporations, controlling almost 30 companies across a wide variety of industries. Its CEO, Carlos Rodríguez-Pastor Jr., inherited the company from his father, a former political exile who, upon his return in 1994, led a consortium that bought one of Peru's largest banks, Banco Internacional del Perú, from the government. Rodríguez-Pastor took control of the bank when his father died, in 1995.

Rodríguez-Pastor wanted to be more than a banker. His ambition was to help transform Peru's economy by building up its middle class. In the newly renamed Interbank he saw an opportunity to both create middle-class jobs and cater to middle-class needs. From the outset, however, he grasped that he couldn't achieve this goal with the "great man" approach to strategy characteristic of the large, family-controlled conglomerates that often dominate emerging economies. Reaching it would take the carefully engineered engagement of many stakeholders.

Seeding a culture of innovation

The first task was making the bank competitive. For ideas, Rodríguez-Pastor decided to look to the leading financial marketplace in his hemisphere, the United States. He persuaded an analyst at a U.S. brokerage house to let him join an investor tour of U.S. banks, even though Interbank wasn't one of the broker's clients.

If he wanted to build a business that could trigger social change, absorbing some insights by himself and bringing them home wouldn't be enough, Rodríguez-Pastor realized. If he simply imposed his own ideas, buy-in would depend largely on his authority—not a context conducive to social transformation. He needed his managers to learn how to develop insights too, so that they could also spot and seize opportunities for advancing his broader ambition. So he talked the analyst into allowing four of his colleagues to join the tour.

This incident was emblematic of his participative approach to strategy making, which enabled Rodríguez-Pastor to build a strong, innovative management team that put the bank on a competitive footing and diversified the company into a range of businesses catering to the middle class: supermarkets, department stores, pharmacies, and cinemas. By 2015 Intercorp, the group built around Interbank, employed some 55,000 people and had projected revenues of $5 billion.

Over the years, Rodríguez-Pastor has expanded his investment in educating the management team. He sent managers each year to programs at top schools and companies (such as Harvard Business School and IDEO) and worked with those institutions to develop new programs for Intercorp, tossing out ideas that didn't work and refining ones that did. Most recently, in conjunction with IDEO, Intercorp launched its own design center, La Victoria Lab. Located in an up-and-coming area of Lima, it serves as the core of a growing urban innovation hub.

But Rodríguez-Pastor didn't stop at creating an innovative business group targeting middle-class consumers. The next step in his plan for social transformation involved moving Intercorp outside the traditional business domain.

From wallets to hearts and minds

Good education is critical to a thriving middle class, but Peru was severely lagging in this department. The country's public schools were lamentable, and the private sector was little better at equipping children for a middle-class future. Unless that changed, a positive cycle of productivity and prosperity was unlikely to emerge. Rodríguez-Pastor concluded that Intercorp would have to enter the education business with a value proposition targeted at middle-class parents.

Winning social acceptability for this venture was the real challenge—one complicated by the fact that education is always a minefield of vested interests. An intervention design, therefore, would be critical to the schools' success. Rodríguez-Pastor worked closely with IDEO to map one out. They began by priming the stakeholders, who might well balk at the idea of a large business group operating schools for children—a controversial proposition even in a business-friendly country like the United States.

Intercorp's first move was starting an award in 2007 for "the teacher who leaves a footprint," given to the best teacher in each of the country's 25 regions. It quickly became famous, in part because every teacher who received it also won a car. This established Intercorp's genuine interest in improving education in Peru and helped pave the way for teachers, civil servants, and parents to accept the idea of a chain of schools owned by the company.

Next, in 2010 Intercorp purchased a small school business called San Felipe Neri, managed by entrepreneur Jorge Yzusqui Chessman. With one school in operation and two more in development, Chessman had plans for growth, but Intercorp's experience in building large-scale businesses in Peru could take the venture far beyond what he envisioned. However, the business would have to reengineer its existing model, which required highly skilled teachers, who were in extremely short supply in Peru. Rodríguez-Pastor brought together managers from his other businesses—a marketing expert from his bank, a facilities expert from his supermarket chain, for instance—with IDEO to create a new model, Innova Schools. It would offer excellent education at a price affordable for middle-class families.

The team launched a six-month human-centered design process. It engaged hundreds of students, teachers, parents, and other stakeholders, exploring their needs and motivations, involving them in testing approaches, and soliciting their feedback on classroom layout and interactions. The result was a technology-enabled model that incorporated platforms such as the U.S. online-education pioneer Khan Academy. In it the teacher was positioned as a facilitator rather than the sole lesson provider.

Intervention Design at Innova

Setting the Stage

Innova Schools launched its initiative to bring affordable education to Peru by holding information sessions on its interactive-learning approach with local parents and students.

September 2011: Designing a New Model

The team began by exploring the lives and motivations of Innova's many stakeholders to find out how it could create a system that would engage teachers, students, and parents.

Final design guidelines were created for the classroom space, the schedule, the teaching methods, and the role of the teacher.

Ideas began to crystallize around a technology-enabled model that shifted the teacher from "sage on stage" to "guide on the side" and would make schools affordable and scalable. Teachers tried out software tools and provided feedback on them.

As that strategy solidified, Innova held many sessions with teachers, parents, and school leaders to get feedback on classroom design, discuss ways the schools would evolve, and invite stakeholders into the process of implementation.

November 2012: Piloting the Program

Full pilots were run in two seventh-grade classrooms in two schools. Teachers were thoroughly trained in the new approach, and the model was repeatedly adapted to address their real-time feedback.

2013–Present: Implementation & Evolution

Today the technology-enabled learning model is being implemented in all 29 of Innova's schools. Innova continues to work with its 940-plus teachers to help them use this new approach. It also regularly runs parent engagement sessions; seeks feedback from teachers, coaches, and students; and iterates on its methodology and curriculum.

The intervention design challenge was that parents might object to having their children learn via laptops in the classroom, and teachers might rebel at the notion of supporting learning rather than leading it. So after six months of preparation, Innova launched a full-scale pilot and brought in parents and teachers to design and run it.

The pilot demonstrated that students, parents, and teachers loved the model, but some of the assumptions were far off base. Parents didn't object to the teaching approach; in fact, they insisted that the laptops not be taken away at the end of the pilot. Additionally, 85% of the students used the laptops outside classroom hours. The model was tweaked on the basis of the insights from the pilot, and both the parents and teachers became huge advocates for the Innova model in nearby locations.

Word of mouth spread, and soon the schools were fully enrolled before they were even built. Because Innova had a reputation for innovation, teachers wanted to work there, even though it paid less than the public system. With 29 schools up and running, Innova is now on track to meet its goal of 70 schools by 2020 and plans to expand into every market in Peru and even markets outside the country.

Spreading the wealth

If it followed conventional business wisdom, Intercorp would have focused on the richer parts of the country's capital, Lima, where a middle class was naturally emerging. But Rodríguez-Pastor recognized that the provinces needed a middle class as well. Fostering one there obviously involved job creation. One way Intercorp could create jobs was to expand its supermarket chain, which it had purchased from Royal Ahold in 2003 and renamed Supermercados Peruanos.

In 2007 the chain began establishing stores in the provinces. Local consumers were certainly receptive to the idea. When one store opened in Huancayo, curious customers queued up for an hour or more to enter it. For many it was their first experience with modern retail. By 2010 the chain was operating 67 supermarkets in nine regions. Today it boasts 102 stores nationwide.

Early on, Intercorp realized that retail ventures of this kind risked impoverishing local communities rather than enriching them. Though a supermarket did provide well-paid jobs, it could hurt the business of local farmers and producers. Since they were small scale and usually operated with low food-safety standards, it would be tempting to source almost everything from Lima. But the logistics costs of doing that would erode profit margins, and if the chain crowded out the local producers, it might destroy more jobs than it created.

Intercorp thus needed to stimulate local production through early engagement with local businesses. In 2010 the company launched the Perú Pasión program, with support from the Corporación Andina de Fomento (an NGO) and Huancayo's regional government. Perú Pasión helps farmers and small manufacturers upgrade their capabilities enough to supply their local Supermercados Peruano. Over time some of these suppliers have even developed into regional or national suppliers in their own right.

Currently, Supermercados Peruanos sources 218 products, representing approximately $1.5 million in annual sales, from Perú Pasión businesses. One is Procesadora de Alimentos Velasquez. Originally a neighborhood bakery serving a few small nearby grocery shops, it began supplying a Supermercados store in 2010, generating just $6,000 in annual sales. Today, thanks to Perú Pasión's help, it supplies three stores for nearly $40,000 in annual sales. Concepción Lacteos, a dairy producer, is another success. In 2010 it began supplying its local Supermercados store for about $2,500 in annual sales. In 2014 it supplied 28 stores, including the chain's upscale outlets in Lima, and generated $100,000 in sales.

Intercorp's success in boosting the middle class in Peru depended on the thoughtful design of many artifacts: a leading-edge bank, an innovative school system, and businesses adapted for frontier towns across Peru. But equally important has been the design of the introduction of these new artifacts into the status quo. Rodríguez-Pastor carefully mapped out the steps necessary to engage all the relevant parties in their adoption. He deepened the skills of the executives on his leadership team, increased the design know-how of his people, won over teachers and parents to the idea that a conglomerate could provide education, and partnered with local producers to build their capacity to supply supermarkets. In conjunction with well-designed artifacts, these carefully designed interventions have made the social transformation of Peru a real possibility rather than an idealistic aspiration.

———————

The principles of this approach are clear and consistent. Intervention is a multistep process—consisting of many small steps, not a few big ones. Along the entire journey interactions with the users of a complex artifact are essential to weeding out bad designs and building confidence in the success of good ones.

Design thinking began as a way to improve the process of designing tangible products. But that's not where it will end. The Intercorp story and others like it show that design-thinking principles have the potential to be even more powerful when applied to managing the intangible challenges involved in getting people to engage with and adopt innovative new ideas and experiences.

Originally published in September 2015. Reprint R1509C

The Innovation Catalysts

by Roger L. Martin

ONE DAY IN 2007, midway through a five-hour PowerPoint presentation, Scott Cook realized that he wasn't another Steve Jobs. At first it was a bitter disappointment. Like many entrepreneurs, Cook wanted the company he had cofounded to be like Apple—design driven, innovation intensive, wowing consumers year in and year out with fantastic offerings. But that kind of success always seemed to need a powerful visionary at the top.

This article is about how Cook and his colleagues at the software development company Intuit found an alternative to the Steve Jobs model: one that has enabled Intuit to become a design-driven innovation machine. Any corporation—no matter how small or prosaic its business—can make the same grassroots transformation if it really wants to.

The Birth of the Idea

Intuit's transformation arguably began in 2004, with its adoption of the famous Net Promoter Score. Developed by Fred Reichheld, of Bain & Company, NPS depends on one simple question for customers: How likely are you, on a scale of 0 (not at all likely) to 10 (extremely likely), to recommend this product or service to a colleague or friend? "Detractors" answer from 0 to 6, "passives" answer 7 or 8, and "promoters" answer 9 or 10. A company's Net Promoter Score is the percentage of promoters less the percentage of detractors.

For the first couple of years, Intuit saw its NPS rise significantly, owing to a number of marketing initiatives. But by 2007 NPS growth had stalled. It was not hard to see why. Although Intuit had lowered its detractor percentage substantially, it had made little headway with promoters. Customer recommendations of new products were especially disappointing.

Clearly, Intuit needed to figure out how to galvanize its customers. Cook, a member of Procter & Gamble's board of directors, approached Claudia Kotchka, then P&G's vice president of design innovation and strategy, for advice. Following their discussions, Cook and Steve Bennett, then Intuit's CEO, decided to focus on the role of design in innovation at a two-day off-site for the company's top 300 managers. Cook created a one-day program on what he called Design for Delight (D4D)—an event aimed at launching Intuit's reinvention as a design-driven company.

The centerpiece of the day was that five-hour PowerPoint presentation, in which Cook laid out the wonders of design and how it could entice Intuit's customers. The managers listened dutifully and clapped appreciatively at the end, as they were supposed to; Cook was, after all, a company founder. Nevertheless, he was disappointed by his reception. Despite some interest in the ideas presented, there was little energy in the room.

But although the main event fell flat, the one that followed did not. Cook had met a young consulting associate professor at Stanford named Alex Kazaks, whom he'd invited to present for an hour at the off-site. Like Cook, Kazaks began with a PowerPoint presentation, but he ended his after 10 minutes and used the rest of the time for a participatory exercise: The managers worked through a design challenge, creating prototypes, getting feedback, iterating, and refining.

The group was mesmerized. Afterward Cook informally polled the participants, asking what takeaways they'd gotten from the daylong session. Two-thirds of the lessons they reported came from

Idea in Brief

A few years ago the software development company Intuit realized that it needed a new approach to galvanizing customers. The company's Net Promoter Score was faltering, and customer recommendations of new products were especially disappointing. Intuit decided to hold a two-day, off-site meeting for the company's top 300 managers with a focus on the role of design in innovation. One of the days was dedicated to a program called Design for Delight. The centerpiece of the day was a PowerPoint presentation by Intuit founder Scott Cook, who realized midway through that he was no Steve Jobs: The managers listened dutifully, but there was little energy in the room. By contrast, a subsequent exercise in which the participants worked through a design challenge by creating prototypes, getting feedback, iterating, and refining, had them mesmerized. The eventual result was the creation of a team of nine design-thinking coaches—"innovation catalysts"—from across Intuit who were made available to help any work group create prototypes, run experiments, and learn from customers. The process includes a "painstorm" (to determine the customer's greatest pain point), a "sol-jam" (to generate and then winnow possible solutions), and a "code-jam" (to write code "good enough" to take to customers within two weeks). Design for Delight has enabled employees throughout Intuit to move from satisfying customers to delighting them.

the hands-on exercise. This reaction made Cook think: He might not be the next Steve Jobs, but perhaps his company didn't need one. Given a few tools, coaching, and practice, could the grass roots of the company drive success in innovation and customer delight?

From Idea to Initiative

Like most Silicon Valley tech companies, Intuit had user-interface designers, graphic designers, and others buried relatively deep in the organization. Cook turned to a particularly talented young design director, Kaaren Hanson, and asked her what she would do to promote design at Intuit.

Hanson realized that the company needed an organized program for moving from talking about D4D to doing it. She persuaded Cook to let her create a team of design-thinking coaches—"innovation catalysts"—who could help Intuit managers work on initiatives throughout the organization. Hanson selected nine colleagues to join her in this role. Their training and deployment was her central agenda for FY 2009.

In selecting the nine, Hanson looked first for people with a broad perspective on what it meant to be a designer: Beyond creating a graphic user interface that was both appealing and intuitive, it included thinking about whether the software solved the user's problem in a delightful way. She wanted her coaches to be interested in talking to users and solving problems with colleagues rather than depending solely on their own genius. If they were to successfully coach others in design thinking, they'd need an outgoing personality and good people skills.

She invited two direct reports from her own business unit and seven people from other units across the company. The group included six women and four men. They came from a variety of fields within Intuit—design, research, product management—and had titles such as user-interface architect, principal researcher, staff designer, and product manager. Hanson chose people who were influential even though they were all one or two levels below director, meaning closer to the bottom of the organization than the top. All nine signed up enthusiastically.

To begin building design thinking into the DNA of the company, Cook and Hanson organized a series of Design for Delight forums. These were typically attended by more than 1,000 employees and featured a speaker who'd had exemplary success in creating customer delight. Half the featured speakers came from inside Intuit; the other half included the founding CEO of Flip Video, Facebook's top data scientist, and the head of Apple Stores. The forums also showcased D4D successes to date and shared best practices. People who worked together were encouraged to attend together and were asked as a team to identify the one thing they would do differently after the forum.

To ensure that managers who were thinking design didn't become too intimidated to begin the process, or frustrated trying to do something with which they had little experience, or delayed by needing to hire an outside design consultant, Hanson's innovation catalysts were available to help any work group create prototypes, run experiments, and learn from customers. Of course, there was a risk that this would stretch the catalysts too thin, so Hanson placed some constraints on their availability. They were expected to spend 25% of their time on big-payoff projects for Intuit overall. Hanson kept in close contact with general managers who had catalysts working with them to make sure that the catalysts were addressing the managers' biggest problems. She realized that if design momentum was to be maintained, her coaches had to be seen as responsible for three or four visible and high-impact wins a year.

Some enabling came from the very bottom of the organization. In 2008 two employees who had been at Intuit only four months designed an online social network for the D4D initiative, which they rolled out the following year with management's consent but without its direct support. In its first year the new platform, named Brainstorm, generated 32 ideas that made it to market.

From Presentations to Experiments

Traditionally, decisions at Intuit had been made on the basis of PowerPoint presentations. Managers would work to produce both (what they saw as) a great product and a great presentation for selling the concept to their bosses. Under this system Intuit managers voted on ideas and then tried to sell them to customers. A key component of D4D, therefore, was shifting the focus away from managerial presentations. It would be far better, Hanson and Cook realized, to learn directly from customers through experiments.

Today D4D innovations begin with what Intuit calls the painstorm—a process developed by two innovation catalysts, Rachel Evans and Kim McNealy. It is aimed at figuring out customers' greatest pain point for which Intuit can provide relief.

Recruiting the Innovation Catalysts

IN 2008 KAAREN HANSON sent this e-mail to some Intuit colleagues:

Subject: Phase II of Design for Delight—we need YOU

You have been nominated (and your participation has been approved by your manager) to help us drive Phase II of Design for Delight at Intuit. You are a critical leader who can enable Intuit to become one of the principal design-thinking cultures. We have a number of levers at our disposal but we need your help to develop even better ideas to drive design thinking deeper into the organization.

Here's what you'll be committing to:

- **Actively participate in a one-day brainstorm/workshop** in early August to work through what we (as a force of design thinking and as a larger company) might do to take Design for Delight to its next level. Scott will come by and respond to our ideas/plan towards the end of the day

- **Commit to the execution of initiatives** generated through the August workshop

- **Become a more visible Design for Delight leader** across Intuit (e.g., help teach a Design for Delight 101 session/workshop to FastPath or some other such leadership session, contribute to the D4D body of knowledge through existing and future contribution systems, be a sounding board for Intuit execs)

- **Be a D4D coach/facilitator** that the larger company can draw upon (e.g., coach key teams across Intuit in brainstorming, design reviews, etc.)

In total, your commitment will be about 2 days/month—and we'll be able to work around your schedule.

Let me know if you are in for FY09—and I'll get the August date on everyone's calendars. Right now, we're looking at an in-person workshop on August 4th, 5th, or 6th in Mountain View.

In a painstorm, team members talk to and observe customers in their offices or homes rather than sit in Intuit offices and imagine what they want. This exercise often shatters preconceptions. Going into one painstorm for a sales-oriented product, the team was convinced that the product concept should be "Grow your business."

But the painstorm showed that "Grow your business" sounded very ambiguous to customers—it could refer to growing revenues from their existing customers (not a pain point for them) or to acquiring similar small businesses (also not a pain point, but expensive). The true pain point was acquiring entirely new customers through organic sales efforts. "Get customers" was a winning concept that focused laserlike on that.

Next, within two weeks, the group holds a "sol-jam," in which people generate concepts for as many product or service solutions as possible to address the pain points they've identified and then weed the concepts down to a short list for prototyping and testing. In the early days of prototyping, these high-potential solutions were integrated into Intuit's software development process. But the innovation catalysts realized that the best way to maintain momentum would be to get code into users' hands as quickly as possible. This would help determine whether the solution had potential and, if so, what needed to be done to enhance it. So the third step became moving immediately to "code-jam," with the goal of writing code that wasn't airtight but was good enough to take to customers within two weeks of the sol-jam. Thus, proceeding from the painstorm to the first user feedback on a new product usually takes only four weeks.

Let's look at a couple of examples. When Intuit's tax group began to think about mobile apps, Carol Howe, a project manager and innovation catalyst, started with the customer. Her five-person team went "out in the wild," she says, to observe dozens of smartphone users. It quickly narrowed in on millennials, whose income range made them likely candidates for the simplest tax experience. The team created multiple concepts and iterated with customers on a weekly basis. They brought customers in each Friday, distilled what they'd learned on Monday, brainstormed concepts on Tuesday, designed them on Wednesday, and coded them on Thursday, before bringing the customers in again. Through these iterations the team uncovered multiple "delighters." They launched a pilot in California in January 2010 and expanded nationwide in January 2011. The resulting application, SnapTax, has 4.5 stars in both the Apple and Android stores and a Net Promoter Score in the high 80s.

An even better example comes from India. In 2008 members of the India team came up with an idea remote from tax preparation and other core Intuit North America products, none of which were likely to succeed in India. The idea, a service for poor Indian farmers, was interesting enough for Intuit to give Deepa Bachu, a long-time development manager, the green light to explore it. Bachu and an engineer spent weeks following subsistence farmers through their daily lives—in the fields, in their villages, and at the markets where they sold their produce. The two came to appreciate the farmers' greatest pain point—perishable inventory that either went unsold or got a suboptimal price. If Intuit could enable the farmers to consistently sell their produce before spoilage and at a decent price, their pain would be reduced or eliminated.

After the painstorm and the sol-jam, the team went into rapid experimentation. Within seven weeks it was running a test of what was eventually launched as Mobile Bazaar, a simple text-messaging-based marketplace connecting buyers and sellers. To get there so fast, the team had cleverly faked parts of the product that would have been costly and slow to code and build. These came to be known as "fako backends." What the user saw looked real, but behind the user interface was a human being—like the Wizard of Oz behind the curtain—rather than thousands of lines of code that would have taken months to write.

The initial trials showed that half the farmers were able to increase their prices by more than 10%; some of them earned as much as 50% more. Within a year of launch, Mobile Bazaar had 180,000 subscribing farmers, most of them acquired by word of mouth. They report that, on average, the service boosts their prices by 16%.

From Breakthroughs to Culture

Hanson was pleased with the progress of the 10 original innovation catalysts in their first year and with the organization's receptivity, but she knew that Intuit would have to scale up to make the transformation complete. Brad Smith, the new CEO, was raising innovation expectations for the whole company, focusing particularly on new arenas that he described as "mobile, social, and global." Hanson set a goal for FY 2010 to select, train, and deploy another 65 catalysts. This meant sourcing from a broader pool of talent—going deeper into product management and engineering—and creating a small dedicated team to support the catalysts and increase D4D pull from mid-level managers.

She appointed Suzanne Pellican, one of the original 10, to expand the catalysts' number and capabilities. Hanson had learned from the initial work that the strongest design thinkers didn't necessarily make the best catalysts. She says, "We not only needed people who were design thinkers—we also needed people with passion to give D4D away and help others to do great work, versus coming up with a great idea and bringing it to others."

The catalysts also needed mutual support. Hanson's team had found that they did their best work when they worked together. They learned new ideas and techniques from one another and provided moral support in tough situations. So as Pellican scaled up the catalyst corps, she made sure that each catalyst was part of an organized "posse" that typically extended across business units, allowing new methods to travel quickly from one end of the organization to the other.

To increase the catalysts' effectiveness, Hanson established a second small team—led by Joseph O'Sullivan, another of the original 10—to help middle management embrace both design thinking as a concept and the innovation catalysts as enablers. For example, after several catalysts reported encountering resistance at the director level, Hanson and O'Sullivan worked to integrate design thinking into Intuit's leadership training programs, applying it directly to problems that leaders faced. In one training program an IT director was challenged to lead a team tasked with reducing company spending on employees' mobile devices by $500,000. O'Sullivan's group held a one-day session on painstorming and soljamming for the team. The IT director achieved the desired saving and won much appreciation from the members of her team for having made their task so much easier than expected. She and the other participants in that leadership training program became fervent D4D advocates.

Encouraging experimentation rather than PowerPoint has enabled employees throughout Intuit to move from satisfying customers to delighting them. Design for Delight has stuck because people see that it is an obviously better and more enjoyable way of innovating.

Innovation activity has increased dramatically in the organization. Take TurboTax, Intuit's single biggest product. In the 2006 tax year the TurboTax unit ran just one customer experiment. In 2010 it ran 600. Experiments in the QuickBooks unit went from a few each year to 40 last year. Intuit now seizes new opportunities more quickly. Brad Smith pushed for D4D-led innovation in the fast-growing arena of mobile apps, and within 24 months the company went from zero to 18, with a number of them, including SnapTax, off to a very successful start. Net Promoter Scores are up across the company, and growth in revenue and income has increased over the past three years.

Scott Cook may not have been another Steve Jobs, but it turned out that Intuit didn't need one.

Originally published in June 2011. Reprint R1106E

Know Your Customers' "Jobs to Be Done"

by Clayton M. Christensen, Taddy Hall, Karen Dillon, and David S. Duncan

FOR AS LONG AS WE CAN REMEMBER, innovation has been a top priority—and a top frustration—for leaders. In a recent McKinsey poll, 84% of global executives reported that innovation was extremely important to their growth strategies, but a staggering 94% were dissatisfied with their organizations' innovation performance. Most people would agree that the vast majority of innovations fall far short of ambitions.

On paper, this makes no sense. Never have businesses known more about their customers. Thanks to the big data revolution, companies now can collect an enormous variety and volume of customer information, at unprecedented speed, and perform sophisticated analyses of it. Many firms have established structured, disciplined innovation processes and brought in highly skilled talent to run them. Most firms carefully calculate and mitigate innovations' risks. From the outside, it looks as if companies have mastered a precise, scientific process. But for most of them, innovation is still painfully hit-or-miss.

What has gone so wrong?

The fundamental problem is, most of the masses of customer data companies create is structured to show correlations: *This customer looks like that one*, or *68% of customers say they prefer version A to version B.* While it's exciting to find patterns in the numbers, they don't mean that one thing actually caused another. And though it's no surprise that correlation isn't causality, we suspect that most managers have grown comfortable basing decisions on correlations.

Why is this misguided? Consider the case of one of this article's coauthors, Clayton Christensen. He's 64 years old. He's six feet eight inches tall. His shoe size is 16. He and his wife have sent all their children off to college. He drives a Honda minivan to work. He has a lot of characteristics, but none of them has caused him to go out and buy the *New York Times.* His reasons for buying the paper are much more specific. He might buy it because he needs something to read on a plane or because he's a basketball fan and it's March Madness time. Marketers who collect demographic or psychographic information about him—and look for correlations with other buyer segments—are not going to capture those reasons.

After decades of watching great companies fail, we've come to the conclusion that the focus on correlation—and on knowing more and more about customers—is taking firms in the wrong direction. What they really need to home in on is the progress that the customer is trying to make in a given circumstance—what the customer hopes to accomplish. This is what we've come to call the *job to be done.*

We all have many jobs to be done in our lives. Some are little (pass the time while waiting in line); some are big (find a more fulfilling career). Some surface unpredictably (dress for an out-of-town business meeting after the airline lost my suitcase); some regularly (pack a healthful lunch for my daughter to take to school). When we buy a product, we essentially "hire" it to help us do a job. If it does the job well, the next time we're confronted with the same job, we tend to hire that product again. And if it does a crummy job, we "fire" it and look for an alternative. (We're using the word "product" here as shorthand for any solution that companies can sell; of course, the full set of "candidates" we consider hiring can often go well beyond just offerings from companies.)

This insight emerged over the past two decades in a course taught by Clay at Harvard Business School. (See "Marketing Malpractice,"

Idea in Brief

What's Wrong

Innovation success rates are shockingly low worldwide, and have been for decades.

What's Needed

Marketers and product developers focus too much on customer profiles and on correlations unearthed in data, and not enough on what customers are trying to achieve in a particular circumstance.

What's Effective

Successful innovators identify poorly performed "jobs" in customers' lives—and then design products, experiences, and processes around those jobs.

HBR, December 2005.) The theory of jobs to be done was developed in part as a complement to the theory of disruptive innovation—which at its core is about competitive responses to innovation: It explains and predicts the behavior of companies in danger of being disrupted and helps them understand which new entrants pose the greatest threats.

But disruption theory doesn't tell you how to create products and services that customers want to buy. Jobs-to-be-done theory does. It transforms our understanding of customer choice in a way that no amount of data ever could, because it gets at the causal driver behind a purchase.

The Business of Moving Lives

A decade ago, Bob Moesta, an innovation consultant and a friend of ours, was charged with helping bolster sales of new condominiums for a Detroit-area building company. The company had targeted downsizers—retirees looking to move out of the family home and divorced single parents. Its units were priced to appeal to that segment—$120,000 to $200,000—with high-end touches to give a sense of luxury. "Squeakless" floors. Triple-waterproof basements. Granite counters and stainless steel appliances. A well-staffed sales team was available six days a week for any prospective buyer who walked in the door. A generous marketing campaign splashed ads across the relevant Sunday real estate sections.

The units got lots of traffic, but few visits ended up converting to sales. Maybe bay windows would be better? Focus group participants thought that sounded good. So the architect scrambled to add bay windows (and any other details that the focus group suggested) to a few showcase units. Still sales did not improve.

Although the company had done a cost-benefit analysis of all the details in each unit, it actually had very little idea what made the difference between a tire kicker and a serious buyer. It was easy to speculate about reasons for poor sales: bad weather, underperforming salespeople, the looming recession, holiday slowdowns, the condos' location. But instead of examining those factors, Moesta took an unusual approach: He set out to learn from the people who had bought units what job they were hiring the condominiums to do. "I asked people to draw a timeline of how they got here," he recalls. The first thing he learned, piecing together patterns in scores of interviews, was what did *not* explain who was most likely to buy. There wasn't a clear demographic or psychographic profile of the new-home buyers, even though all were downsizers. Nor was there a definitive set of features that buyers valued so much that it tipped their decisions.

But the conversations revealed an unusual clue: the dining room table. Prospective customers repeatedly told the company they wanted a big living room, a large second bedroom for visitors, and a breakfast bar to make entertaining easy and casual; on the other hand, they didn't need a formal dining room. And yet, in Moesta's conversations with actual buyers, the dining room table came up repeatedly. "People kept saying, 'As soon as I figured out what to do with my dining room table, then I was free to move,'" reports Moesta. He and his colleagues couldn't understand why the dining room table was such a big deal. In most cases people were referring to well-used, out-of-date furniture that might best be given to charity—or relegated to the local dump.

But as Moesta sat at his own dining room table with his family over Christmas, he suddenly understood. Every birthday was spent around that table. Every holiday. Homework was spread out on it. The table represented family.

What was stopping buyers from making the decision to move, he hypothesized, was not a feature that the construction company had failed to offer but rather the anxiety that came with giving up something that had profound meaning. The decision to buy a six-figure condo, it turned out, often hinged on a family member's willingness to take custody of a clunky piece of used furniture.

That realization helped Moesta and his team begin to grasp the struggle potential home buyers faced. "I went in thinking we were in the business of new-home construction," he recalls. "But I realized we were in the business of moving lives."

With this understanding of the job to be done, dozens of small but important changes were made to the offering. For example, the architect managed to create space in the units for a dining room table by reducing the size of the second bedroom. The company also focused on easing the anxiety of the move itself: It provided moving services, two years' worth of storage, and a sorting room within the condo development where new owners could take their time making decisions about what to discard.

The insight into the job the customers needed done allowed the company to differentiate its offering in ways competitors weren't likely to copy—or even comprehend. The new perspective changed everything. The company actually raised prices by $3,500, which included (profitably) covering the cost of moving and storage. By 2007, when industry sales were off by 49% and the market was plummeting, the developers had actually grown business by 25%.

Getting a Handle on the Job to Be Done

Successful innovations help consumers to solve problems—to make the progress they need to, while addressing any anxieties or inertia that might be holding them back. But we need to be clear: "Job to be done" is not an all-purpose catchphrase. Jobs are complex and multifaceted; they require precise definition. Here are some principles to keep in mind:

"Job" is shorthand for what an individual really seeks to accomplish in a given circumstance
But this goal usually involves more than just a straightforward task; consider the experience a person is trying to create. What the condo buyers sought was to transition into a new life, in the specific circumstance of downsizing—which is completely different from the circumstance of buying a first home.

The *circumstances* are more important than customer characteristics, product attributes, new technologies, or trends
Before they understood the underlying job, the developers focused on trying to make the condo units ideal. But when they saw innovation through the lens of the customers' circumstances, the competitive playing field looked totally different. For example, the new condos were competing not against other new condos but against the idea of no move at all.

Good innovations solve problems that formerly had only inadequate solutions—or no solution
Prospective condo buyers were looking for simpler lives without the hassles of home ownership. But to get that, they thought, they had to endure the stress of selling their current homes, wading through exhausting choices about what to keep. Or they could stay where they were, even though that solution would become increasingly imperfect as they aged. It was only when given a third option that addressed all the relevant criteria that shoppers became buyers.

Jobs are never simply about function—they have powerful social and emotional dimensions
Creating space in the condo for a dining room table reduced a very real anxiety that prospective buyers had. They could take the table with them if they couldn't find a home for it. And having two years' worth of storage and a sorting room on the premises gave condo buyers permission to work slowly through the emotions involved in deciding what to keep and what to discard. Reducing their stress made a catalytic difference.

These principles are described here in a business-to-consumer context, but jobs are just as important in B2B settings. For an example, see the sidebar "Doing Jobs for B2B Customers."

Designing Offerings Around Jobs

A deep understanding of a job allows you to innovate without guessing what trade-offs your customers are willing to make. It's a kind of job spec.

Of the more than 20,000 new products evaluated in Nielsen's 2012–2016 Breakthrough Innovation report, only 92 had sales of more than $50 million in year one and sustained sales in year two, excluding close-in line extensions. (Coauthor Taddy Hall is the lead author of Nielsen's report.) On the surface the list of hits might seem random—International Delight Iced Coffee, Hershey's Reese's Minis, and Tidy Cats Lightweight, to name just a few—but they have one thing in common. According to Nielsen, every one of them nailed a poorly performed and very specific job to be done. International Delight Iced Coffee let people enjoy in their homes the taste of coffeehouse iced drinks they'd come to love. And thanks to Tidy Cats Lightweight litter, millions of cat owners no longer had to struggle with getting heavy, bulky boxes off store shelves, into car trunks, and up the stairs into their homes.

How did Hershey's achieve a breakout success with what might seem to be just another version of the decades-old peanut butter cup? Its researchers began by exploring the circumstances in which Reese's enthusiasts were "firing" the current product formats. They discovered an array of situations—driving the car, standing in a crowded subway, playing a video game—in which the original large format was too big and messy, while the smaller, individually wrapped cups were a hassle (opening them required two hands). In addition, the accumulation of the cups' foil wrappers created a guilt-inducing tally of consumption: *I had* that *many?* When the company focused on the job that smaller versions of Reese's were being hired to do, it created Reese's Minis. They have no foil wrapping to leave a telltale trail, and they come in a resealable flat-bottom bag

Identifying Jobs to Be Done

JOBS ANALYSIS DOESN'T REQUIRE YOU to throw out the data and research you've already gathered. Personas, ethnographic research, focus groups, customer panels, competitive analysis, and so on can all be perfectly valid starting points for surfacing important insights. Here are five questions for uncovering jobs your customers need help with.

Do You Have a Job That Needs to Be Done?

In a data-obsessed world, it might be a surprise that some of the greatest innovators have succeeded with little more than intuition to guide their efforts. Pleasant Rowland saw the opportunity for American Girl dolls when searching for gifts that would help her connect with her nieces. Sheila Marcelo started Care.com, the online "matchmaking" service for child care, senior care, and pet care, after struggling with her family's own care needs. Now, less than 10 years later, it boasts more than 19 million members across 16 countries and revenues approaching $140 million.

Where Do You See Nonconsumption?

You can learn as much from people who aren't hiring any product as from those who are. Nonconsumption is often where the most fertile opportunities lie, as one university found when it reached out to older learners.

What Work-Arounds Have People Invented?

If you see consumers struggling to get something done by cobbling together work-arounds, pay attention. They're probably deeply unhappy with the

that a consumer can easily dip a single hand into. The results were astounding: $235 million in the first two years' sales and the birth of a breakthrough category extension.

Creating customer experiences

Identifying and understanding the job to be done are only the first steps in creating products that customers want—especially ones they will pay premium prices for. It's also essential to create the right set of experiences for the purchase and use of the product and then integrate those experiences into a company's processes.

When a company does that, it's hard for competitors to catch up. Take American Girl dolls. If you don't have a preteen girl in your life, you may not understand how anyone could pay more than a available solutions—and a promising base of new business. When Intuit noticed that small-business owners were using Quicken—designed for individuals—to do accounting for their firms, it realized small firms represented a major new market.

What Tasks Do People Want to Avoid?

There are plenty of jobs in daily life that we'd just as soon get out of. We call these "negative jobs." Harvard Business School alum Rick Krieger and some partners decided to start QuickMedx, the forerunner of CVS MinuteClinics, after Krieger spent a frustrating few hours waiting in an emergency room for his son to get a strep-throat test. MinuteClinics can see walk-in patients instantly, and their nurse practitioners can prescribe medicines for routine ailments, such as conjunctivitis, ear infections, and strep throat.

What Surprising Uses Have Customers Invented for Existing Products?

Recently, some of the biggest successes in consumer packaged goods have resulted from a job identified through unusual uses of established products. For example, NyQuil had been sold for decades as a cold remedy, but it turned out that some consumers were knocking back a couple of spoonfuls to help them sleep, even when they weren't sick. Hence, ZzzQuil was born, offering consumers the good night's rest they wanted without the other active ingredients they didn't need.

hundred dollars for a doll and shell out hundreds more for clothing, books, and accessories. Yet to date the business has sold 29 million dolls, and it racks up more than $500 million in sales annually.

What's so special about American Girls? Well, it's not the dolls themselves. They come in a variety of styles and ethnicities and are lovely, sturdy dolls. They're *nice*, but they aren't *amazing*. Yet for nearly 30 years they have dominated their market. When you see a product or service that no one has successfully copied, the product itself is rarely the source of the long-term competitive advantage.

American Girl has prevailed for so long because it's not really selling dolls: It's selling an experience. Individual dolls represent different times and places in U.S. history and come with books that relate each doll's backstory. For girls, the dolls provide a rich opportunity to engage their imaginations, connect with friends who also own the dolls, and create unforgettable memories with their mothers and grandmothers. For parents—the buyers—the dolls help engage their daughters in a conversation about the generations of women that came before them—about their struggles, their strength, their values and traditions.

American Girl founder Pleasant Rowland came up with the idea when shopping for Christmas presents for her nieces. She didn't want to give them hypersexualized Barbies or goofy Cabbage Patch Kids aimed at younger children. The dolls—and their worlds—reflect Rowland's nuanced understanding of the job preteen girls hire the dolls to do: help articulate their feelings and validate who they are—their identity, their sense of self, and their cultural and racial background—and make them feel they can surmount the challenges in their lives.

There are dozens of American Girl dolls representing a broad cross section of profiles. Kaya, for example, is a young girl from a Northwest Native American tribe in the late 18th century. Her backstory tells of her leadership, compassion, courage, and loyalty. There's Kirsten Larson, a Swedish immigrant who settles in the Minnesota territory and faces hardships and challenges but triumphs in the end. And so on. A significant part of the allure is the well-written, historically accurate books about each character's life.

Rowland and her team thought through every aspect of the experience required to perform the job. The dolls were never sold in traditional toy stores. They were available only through mail order or at American Girl stores, which were initially located in just a few major metropolitan areas. The stores have doll hospitals that can repair tangled hair or fix broken parts. Some have restaurants in which parents, children, and their dolls can enjoy a kid-friendly menu—or where parents can host birthday parties. A trip to the American Girl store has become a special day out, making the dolls a catalyst for family experiences that will be remembered forever.

No detail was too small to consider. Take the sturdy red-and-pink boxes the dolls come in. Rowland remembers the debate over whether to wrap them with narrow cardboard strips, known as "belly bands." Because the bands each added 2 cents and 27 seconds to the packaging process, the designers suggested skipping them. Rowland says she rejected the idea out of hand: "I said, 'You're not getting it. What has to happen to make this special to the child? I don't want her to see some shrink-wrapped thing coming out of the box. The fact that she has to wait just a split second to get the band off and open the tissue under the lid makes it exciting to open the box. It's not the same as walking down the aisle in the toy store and picking a Barbie off the shelf.'"

In recent years Toys "R" Us, Walmart, and even Disney have all tried to challenge American Girl's success with similar dolls—at a small fraction of the price. Though American Girl, which was acquired by Mattel, has experienced some sales declines in the past two years, to date no competitor has managed to make a dent in its market dominance. Why? Rowland thinks that competitors saw themselves in the "doll business," whereas she never lost sight of why the dolls were cherished: the experiences and stories and connections that they enable.

Aligning processes

The final piece of the puzzle is processes—how the company integrates across functions to support the job to be done. Processes are often hard to see, but they matter profoundly. As MIT's Edgar Schein has discussed, processes are a critical part of an organization's unspoken culture. They tell people inside the company, "This is what matters most to us." Focusing processes on the job to be done provides clear guidance to everyone on the team. It's a simple but powerful way of making sure a company doesn't unintentionally abandon the insights that brought it success in the first place.

A good case in point is Southern New Hampshire University, which has been lauded by *U.S. News & World Report* (and other publications) as one of the most innovative colleges in America. After enjoying a 34% compounded annual growth rate for six years, SNHU was closing in on $535 million in annual revenues at the end of fiscal 2016.

Like many similar academic institutions, SNHU once struggled to find a way to distinguish itself and survive. The university's longtime bread-and-butter strategy had relied on appealing to a

Doing Jobs for B2B Customers

DES TRAYNOR IS A COFOUNDER OF INTERCOM, which makes software that helps companies stay in touch with customers via their websites, mobile apps, e-mail, and Facebook Messenger.

Intercom, which now has more than 10,000 customers and grew fourfold in 2015, adopted a jobs-to-be-done perspective to clarify its strategy in 2011, when it was still an early-stage startup. Traynor spoke about that experience with Derek van Bever and Laura Day of Harvard Business School's Forum for Growth & Innovation. Here is an edited version of their conversation.

FORUM: How did you come across the "jobs" approach to innovation and strategy?

TRAYNOR: Somewhat by accident! In 2011 Intercom had just four engineers and some modest VC backing. I was asked to speak about managing a start up at a conference. Clay Christensen opened the conference and mentioned "jobs to be done."

And that made an impression because . . . ?

We were searching for direction at the time. We knew we wanted to help internet companies talk to their customers—and to make that personal. We knew that the features we shipped were valuable—but we didn't really know who was using us. Customer support? Marketing? Market research? Nor did we know exactly what they were using us for.

How had you approached those questions until then?

We were using a personas-based approach to segmentation, but it wasn't working. We had too many "typical users" who had little in common, going by traits like demographics or job titles. Because we didn't really understand why people were coming to the platform—what they were using it for—we charged a single price for access to the entire platform.

As soon as I grasped the distinction between "customers" and "problems people need help with," a lightbulb went off. I called my cofounder Eoghan McCabe and said, "We're going to build a company that is focused on doing a job."

And how did you figure out what the relevant job was?

We got in touch with innovation consultant Bob Moesta, who has a lot of practical experience with this approach. Bob and his team conducted individual interviews with two types of customers: people who had recently signed on with us, and people who had dropped the service or changed their usage significantly.

He wanted to understand the timeline of events that led up to a purchasing decision and the "forces" that ultimately pushed people into that decision. Bob has a theory that customers always experience conflict when considering a new purchase—what he calls "the struggling moment." There are pressures pushing them to act—to solve a problem by "hiring" a solution—and forces like inertia, fear of change, and anxiety holding them back. His overall objective was to explain, in the customers' words, what caused people to resolve the conflict and "hire" Intercom, and then how well Intercom performed.

I listened in on four interviews live—and tried not to jump to judgment. Two things stood out. One, prospective clients who sampled our services were usually flailing. Their growth had flattened, and they were ready to try something new. And two, the words they described our product with were really different from the words we used. People using it to sign up new customers kept using the word "engage," for example. We used the term "outbound messaging," which has a very different feel.

According to Bob, this is really common: Companies fall in love with their own jargon. They focus on the technology being offered rather than the value being delivered.

What did you learn about the jobs you were being hired to do?

It turned out that people had four distinct jobs: First, help me observe. Show me the people who use my product and what they do with it. Second, help me engage—to convert sign-ups into active users. Third, help me learn— give me rich feedback from the right people. And finally, help me support—to fix my customers' problems.

How much did you change the business once you understood the different jobs your customers had?

A lot. We now offer four distinct services, each designed to support one of those jobs. Our R&D group—120 people—has four teams, one for each job, and we've gone deeper and deeper on each job.

Essentially, we realized that we'd been offering a one-size-fits-none service. The initial price felt high because no customer needed everything we were selling.

How did that change work out?

Our conversion rate has increased, since prospects can now buy just the piece of the site that suits their initial job, and we're able to establish multiple points of sale across client organizations, since there is now a logical path for relationship growth.

traditional student body: 18-year-olds, fresh out of high school, continuing their education. Marketing and outreach were generic, targeting everyone, and so were the policies and delivery models that served the school.

SNHU had an online "distance learning" academic program that was "a sleepy operation on a nondescript corner of the main campus," as president Paul LeBlanc describes it. Yet it had attracted a steady stream of students who wanted to resume an aborted run at a college education. Though the online program was a decade old, it was treated as a side project, and the university put almost no resources into it.

On paper, both traditional and online students might look similar. A 35-year-old and an 18-year-old working toward an accounting degree need the same courses, right? But LeBlanc and his team saw that the job the online students were hiring SNHU to do had almost nothing in common with the job that "coming of age" undergraduates hired the school to do. On average, online students are 30 years old, juggling work and family, and trying to squeeze in an education. Often they still carry debt from an earlier college experience. They're not looking for social activities or a campus scene. They need higher education to provide just four things: convenience, customer service, credentials, and speedy completion times. That, the team realized, presented an enormous opportunity.

SNHU's online program was in competition not with local colleges but with other national online programs, including those offered by both traditional colleges and for-profit schools like the University of Phoenix and ITT Technical Institute. Even more significantly, SNHU was competing with *nothing*. Nonconsumption. Suddenly, the market that had seemed finite and hardly worth fighting for became one with massive untapped potential.

But very few of SNHU's existing policies, structures, and processes were set up to support the actual job that online students needed done. What had to change? "Pretty much everything," LeBlanc recalls. Instead of treating online learning as a second-class citizen, he and his team made it their focus. During a session with about 20 faculty members and administrators, they charted the entire admissions process on a whiteboard. "It looked like a schematic from a nuclear submarine!" he says. The team members circled all the hurdles that SNHU was throwing up—or not helping people overcome—in that process. And then, one by one, they eliminated those hurdles and replaced them with experiences that would satisfy the job that online students needed to get done. Dozens of decisions came out of this new focus.

Here are some key questions the team worked through as it redesigned SNHU's processes:

What experiences will help customers make the progress they're seeking in a given circumstance?

For older students, information about financial aid is critical; they need to find out if continuing their education is even possible, and time is of the essence. Often they're researching options late at night, after a long day, when the kids have finally gone to sleep. So responding to a prospective student's inquiry with a generic e-mail 24 hours later would often miss the window of opportunity. Understanding the context, SNHU set an internal goal of a follow-up phone call within eight and a half minutes. The swift personal response makes prospective students much more likely to choose SNHU.

What obstacles must be removed?

Decisions about a prospect's financial aid package and how much previous college courses would count toward an SNHU degree were resolved within days instead of weeks or months.

What are the social, emotional, and functional dimensions of the job?

Ads for the online program were completely reoriented toward later-life learners. They attempted to resonate not just with the functional dimensions of the job, such as getting the training needed to advance in a career, but also with the emotional and social ones, such as the pride people feel in earning their degrees. One ad featured an SNHU bus roaming the country handing out large framed diplomas to online students who couldn't be on campus for graduation. "Who did you get this degree for?" the voice-over asks, as the commercial captures glowing graduates in their homes. "I got it for me," one woman says, hugging her diploma. "I did this for my mom," beams a 30-something man. "I did it for you, bud," one father says, holding back tears as his young son chirps, "Congratulations, Daddy!"

But perhaps most important, SNHU realized that enrolling prospects in their first class was only the beginning of doing the job. The school sets up each new online student with a personal adviser, who stays in constant contact—and notices red flags even before the students might. This support is far more critical to continuing education students than traditional ones, because so many obstacles in their everyday lives conspire against them. Haven't checked out this week's assignment by Wednesday or Thursday? Your adviser will touch base with you. The unit test went badly? You can count on a call from your adviser to see not only what's going on with the class but what's going on in your life. Your laptop is causing you problems? An adviser might just send you a new one. This unusual level of assistance is a key reason that SNHU's online programs have extremely high Net Promoter Scores (9.6 out of 10) and a graduation rate—about 50%—topping that of virtually every community college (and far above that of costlier, for-profit rivals, which have come under fire for low graduation rates).

SNHU has been open with would-be competitors, offering tours and visits to executives from other educational institutions. But the experiences and processes the university has created for online students would be difficult to copy. SNHU did not invent all its tactics. But what it has done, with laser focus, is ensure that its hundreds and hundreds of processes are tailored to the job students are hiring the school for.

———————

Many organizations have unwittingly designed innovation processes that produce inconsistent and disappointing outcomes. They spend time and money compiling data-rich models that make them masters of description but failures at prediction. But firms don't have to continue down that path. Innovation can be far more predictable—and far more profitable—if you start by identifying jobs that customers are struggling to get done. Without that lens, you're doomed to hit-or-miss innovation. With it, you can leave relying on luck to your competitors.

Originally published in September 2016. Reprint R1609D

Note

This chapter is adapted from *Competing Against Luck: The Story of Innovation and Customer Choice* and is reprinted with the permission of HarperBusiness.

Engineering Reverse Innovations

by Amos Winter and Vijay Govindarajan

SLOWLY BUT STEADILY, IT'S dawning on Western multinationals that it may be a good idea to design products and services in developing economies and, after adding some global tweaks, export them to developed countries.

This process, called "reverse innovation" because it's the opposite of the traditional approach of creating products for advanced economies first, allows companies to enjoy the best of both worlds. It was first described six years ago in an HBR article cowritten by one of the authors of this article, Vijay Govindarajan.

But despite the inexorable logic of reverse innovation, only a few multinationals—notably Coca-Cola, GE, Harmon, Microsoft, Nestlé, PepsiCo, Procter & Gamble, Renault, and Levi Strauss—have succeeded in crafting products in emerging markets and selling them worldwide. Even emerging giants—such as Jain Irrigation, Mahindra & Mahindra, and the Tata Group—have found it tough to create offerings that catch on in both kinds of markets.

For three years now we've been studying this challenge, analyzing more than 35 reverse innovation projects started by multinationals. Our research suggests that the problem stems from a failure to grasp the unique economic, social, and technical contexts of emerging markets. At most Western companies, product developers, who spend a lifetime creating offerings for people similar to themselves, lack a visceral understanding of emerging market consumers, whose spending habits, use of technologies, and perceptions of status are very different. Executives have trouble figuring out how to overcome the constraints of emerging markets—or take advantage of the freedoms they offer. Unable to find the way forward, they tend to fall into one or more mental traps that prevent them from successfully developing reverse innovations.

Our study also shows that executives can avoid these traps by adhering to certain design principles, which together provide a road map for reverse innovation. We distilled them partly from our work with multinationals and partly from the firsthand experiences of a team of MIT engineers led by this article's other author, Amos Winter. His team spent six years designing an off-road wheelchair for people in developing countries, which is now manufactured in India. Called the Leveraged Freedom Chair (LFC), it is 80% faster and 40% more efficient to propel than a conventional wheelchair, and it sells for approximately $250—on par with other developing world wheelchairs. The technologies that generate its high performance and low cost have been incorporated into a Western version, the GRIT Freedom Chair, which was modified with consumer feedback and sells in the United States for $3,295—less than half the price of competing products.

As we will show in the following pages, the reverse innovation process succeeds when engineering creatively intersects with strategy. Companies can capture business opportunities only when they design appropriate products or services and understand the business case for them. That's why it took two academics—one teaching mechanical engineering, and the other strategy—to come up with the principles that must guide the creation of reverse innovations.

Five Traps—and How to Avoid Them

For every product, multinational companies typically produce three variations: a top-of-the-line offering, which provides the best performance at a premium price; a "better" version, which delivers 80% of that performance at 80% of the price; and a "good" variant,

Idea in Brief

The Problem

Multinational companies are starting to realize that developing new products in and for emerging markets will allow them to outperform local rivals and undercut them on price—and even disrupt Western markets. However, most struggle to create those products and then sell them in the developed world.

The Analysis

A three-year study suggests that Western companies often fail to grasp the economic, social, and technical contexts of emerging markets. Most Western product engineers find it tough to overcome these markets' constraints and leverage their flexibility. They tend to fall into one or more traps that thwart their innovation efforts.

The Takeaways

Companies can avoid these traps if they:

1. Define the problem independent of solutions.

2. Create the optimal solution using the design flexibility available.

3. Understand the technical landscape behind the problem.

4. Test products with as many stakeholders as possible.

5. Use constraints to create global winners.

which provides 70% and costs 70% as much. To break into emerging markets, where consumers have very high expectations but much smaller pocketbooks, multinationals usually follow a design philosophy that minimizes the up-front risks: They value-engineer the "good" product, watering it down to a "fair" one that offers 50% of the performance at 50% of the price.

This rarely works. In developing countries, not only do "fair" (or "good enough") products prove too expensive for the middle class, but the upmarket consumers—who can afford them—will prefer the top-of-the-line versions. Meanwhile, because of economies of scale and the globalization of supply chains, local companies are now bringing out high-value products, at relatively cheap prices, more quickly than they used to. Consequently, most multinationals capture only small slivers of the local market.

To win over consumers in developing countries, multinationals' products and services must match or beat the performance of existing ones but at a lower cost. In other words, they must provide 100% of the performance at 10% of the price, as product developers wryly put it. Only through the creation of such disruptive products and technologies can companies both outperform local rivals and undercut them on price. But the traps we mentioned earlier prevent companies from meeting this challenge. To escape those traps, they must follow five design principles.

Trap 1: Trying to match market segments to existing products
Current offerings and processes cast a long shadow when multinationals start creating products for developing countries. At first it appears to be quicker, cheaper, and less risky to adapt an existing product than to develop one from scratch. The idea that time-tested products, with modifications, won't appeal to lower-income customers is difficult to digest. Designers struggle to get away from existing technologies.

The U.S. tractor-manufacturer John Deere, a seasoned global player, encountered this problem in India. There Deere initially sold tractors it had carefully modified for emerging markets. But its small tractors had a wide turning radius, because they had been designed for America's large farms. Indian holdings are very small and close to one another, so farmers there prefer tractors that can make narrow turns. Only after John Deere designed ab initio a tractor for the local market did it taste success in India.

Design principle 1: Define the problem independent of solutions
Casting off preconceived solutions before you set down to define problems will help your company avoid the first trap—and spot opportunities outside its existing product portfolio. Consider the problem of irrigating farms in emerging markets. Farmers will argue for the expansion of the power grid so that they can use electricity to run water pumps and irrigate fields. However, farmers need water, not electricity, and the real requirement is getting water to crops— not power to pumps. If they isolate the problem, engineers may find

that creating ponds near fields or using solar-powered pumps is more cost-effective and environmentally appropriate than expanding the power grid.

When defining problems, executives must keep their eyes and ears open for behavior that may signal needs that customers haven't articulated. In 2002, Commonwealth Telecommunications Organisation researchers reported that in East Africa, people were transferring airtime to family and friends in villages, who were then using or reselling it. Doing so allowed workers in cities to get money to people back home without making long and unsafe journeys with large amounts of cash. It indicated a latent demand for money remittance services. That's how M-Pesa, the successful mobile money-transfer service, was born.

It's good to study the global market in-depth before kicking off the design process. For example, when the MIT team analyzed the wheelchair market, it learned that of the 40 million people with disabilities who didn't have wheelchairs, 70% lived in rural areas where rough roads and muddy paths were often the only links to education, employment, markets, and the community. Environmental conditions were harsh; traditional wheelchairs broke down quickly as a result and were difficult to repair. Because of their poverty, most people got wheelchairs free or at subsidized prices from NGOs, religious organizations, or government agencies. Those suppliers were willing to pay $250 to $350 for a wheelchair—an important price constraint.

No wheelchair user specified the mobility solution he or she desired; the team had to figure out the needs of the market by watching and listening. For inspiration, it drew on the numerous complaints it heard: Wheelchairs were tough to push on village roads; manually powered tricycles were too big to use indoors; imported wheelchairs couldn't be repaired in villages; the commute to an office was often more than a mile, so it was tiring. And so on.

The team's assessment of consumer needs generated four core design requirements:

1. A price of approximately $250

2. A travel range of three miles a day over varied terrain

Key advantages of the Leveraged Freedom Chair

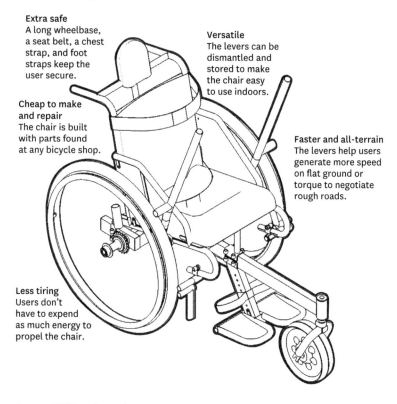

Extra safe
A long wheelbase, a seat belt, a chest strap, and foot straps keep the user secure.

Versatile
The levers can be dismantled and stored to make the chair easy to use indoors.

Cheap to make and repair
The chair is built with parts found at any bicycle shop.

Faster and all-terrain
The levers help users generate more speed on flat ground or torque to negotiate rough roads.

Less tiring
Users don't have to expend as much energy to propel the chair.

Source: GRIT/Asme Demand

3. Indoor usability and maneuverability

4. Easy, low-cost maintenance and local repair

Those criteria conveyed little about what form the wheelchair would have to take. However, had the team missed one of them, imposed an existing solution, or made its own assumptions, it probably would have failed.

Trap 2: Trying to reduce the price by eliminating features
Many multinationals think this is the way to make products afford-able for consumers in emerging markets. People in developing countries are willing to accept lower quality and products based on sunset technologies, runs the argument. This approach often leads to poor decisions and bad product designs.

For example, when one of the Big Three automobile makers decided to enter India in the mid-1990s, it charged its product developers in Detroit with coming up with a suitable model. The designers took an existing mid-price car and eliminated what they felt were unnecessary features for India, including power windows in the rear doors. The new model's price was within the reach of Indians at the top of the pyramid—who hire chauffeurs. Thus the chauffeurs got power windows up front while the owners had to hand-crank the rear windows, greatly reducing customer satisfaction.

Design principle 2: Create an optimal solution, not a watered-down one, using the design freedoms available in emerging markets
Though emerging markets have many constraints, they offer intrin-sic design freedoms as well. These freedoms take various forms: In Egypt high irradiance makes solar power attractive in areas with unreliable power; in India low labor costs and high material costs make manual fabrication cost-effective. Even behavioral differences broaden companies' options: Some African consumers prioritize the purchase of TV sets over roofs, suggesting that companies must appeal to users' wants as well as their needs.

Carefully considering design freedoms helped the MIT team achieve many objectives. For instance, wheelchairs that use a mechanical system of multiple gears, just as geared bicycles do, were available in the developing world, but they were very expen-sive, and few could afford them. Compelled to devise an alternative, the engineers homed in on people's ability to make a broad range of arm movements as something they could use in the drivetrain to make the chair go faster or slower. While that ability isn't specific to emerging markets, the engineers wouldn't have thought of using it if they weren't trying to achieve high performance at a low price—a requirement specific to emerging markets.

The MIT team designed the LFC with two long levers that are pushed to propel the chair; users change speed by shifting the position of their hands on the levers. To go up a hill, users grab high on the levers and gain more leverage; in "low gear" the levers provide 50% more torque than pushing the rims of the chair does. On a flat road, they grab low and push through a larger angle to move faster, generating speeds that are 75% faster than a standard wheelchair's. To brake, users pull back on the levers.

By making the users the machines' most complex part—they are both the power source and the gearbox—the team could fabricate the drivetrain from a simple, single-speed assembly of bicycle parts. In fact, the ability to use bicycle parts was another freedom the team could exploit. People in developing countries use bicycles extensively, and repair shops that stock spare parts are almost everywhere. Incorporating bicycle parts into the drivetrain made the LFC low cost, sustainable, and easy to repair, especially in remote villages.

Trap 3: Forgetting to think through all the technical requirements of emerging markets

When designing offerings for the developing world, engineers assume they're dealing with the same technical landscape that they are in the developed world. But while the laws of science may be the same everywhere, the technical infrastructure is very different in emerging markets. Engineers must understand the technical factors behind problems there—the physics, the chemistry, the energetics, the ecology, and so on—and conduct rigorous analyses to determine the viability of possible solutions.

Thorough calculations will allow engineers to validate or refute assumptions about the market. Consider the PlayPump, designed for Africa, which pumps water from the ground into a tower by harnessing the energy of village children pushing a merry-go-round. Having children do something useful for the community while playing is a win-win by any yardstick. Moreover, a first-order engineering analysis suggested that the technological assumptions were logical.

U.S.-focused upgrades to the GRIT Freedom Chair

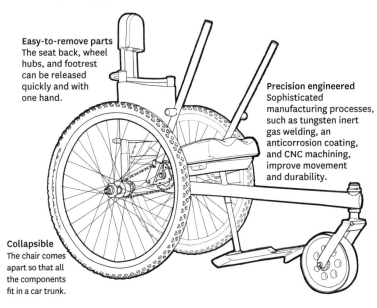

Easy-to-remove parts
The seat back, wheel hubs, and footrest can be released quickly and with one hand.

Precision engineered
Sophisticated manufacturing processes, such as tungsten inert gas welding, an anticorrosion coating, and CNC machining, improve movement and durability.

Collapsible
The chair comes apart so that all the components fit in a car trunk.

Source: GRIT/Nathan Cooke

Let's assume that in a 1,000-strong village, each person needs three liters of drinking water a day, the village has a tower that can hold 3,000 liters, and it's 10 meters high. Using high school physics, one can calculate that 25 children, playing for 10 minutes each, could theoretically fill the tower.

But further analysis alters the picture. After all, children spin merry-go-rounds so that they can ride them until they're dizzy, and if all the energy from their pushing goes to pumping water, the merry-go-round will stop as soon as they stop pushing. That's no fun! If we assume that half their energy goes into spinning and half into pumping, the energy requirement doubles; 50 children must use the PlayPump for 10 minutes each daily to keep the tower full.

If the water comes from a well 10 meters deep, double the energy will be necessary and 100 children must use the merry-go-round. Accounting for inefficiencies, the number could go to 200. What happens when it's too hot, wet, or cold, and children don't want to play on the PlayPump? How will the village get its water then? If the makers of the PlayPump had included all those factors in their calculations, they would have realized it wasn't a technically viable solution. Despite receiving the World Bank Development Marketplace award in 2000 and donor pledges of $16.4 million in 2006, PlayPumps International had stopped installing new units by 2010. The PlayPump sounded like a good idea, but a village water system needs reliable power—and ensuring that isn't child's play.

Design principle 3: Analyze the technical landscape behind the consumer problem

Underlying technical relationships may look markedly different in developing countries. For example, urban Indian homes receive water from pressurized municipal supply systems, just like those found in the United States, which ensure that if there is a leak, water goes out but contaminants can't get in. However, most Indian households use booster pumps to suck water from the municipal pipes to rooftop tanks. This suction pulls contaminants from the ground into the pipes, creating a mechanism for contamination that is not common in the United States.

Social and economic factors often drive the technical requirements for products. For instance, if a company wants to sell inexpensive tractors to low-income farmers, it must make them light; material costs determine much of a tractor's price. Engineers then must check how lowering the weight would affect the machine's performance, particularly traction and pulling force. The latter is important; in emerging markets, farmers use tractors not only to farm but for odd jobs, such as transporting people.

By studying the technical landscape, engineers can identify pain points as well as creative paths around them. Understanding the requirements for energy, force, heat transfer, and so on will illuminate novel ways of satisfying them. As noted earlier, the LFC is human powered, which eliminates the costs of a motor and an energy source. However, the design team had to figure out how users' upper body strength could provide propulsion. It did so by calculating the power and force that people could produce with their arms and the amounts needed on various kinds of terrain. Finally, the designers worked out the optimal length of the two levers so that users could travel at peak efficiency across normal terrain and have enough strength to propel their way out of trouble in harsh conditions such as mud or sand.

Trap 4: Neglecting stakeholders

Many multinationals seem to think that all they need to do to educate product designers about consumers' needs and desires is to parachute them into an emerging market for a few days; drive them around a couple of cities, villages, and slums; and allow them to observe the locals. Those perceptions will be enough to develop products that people will purchase, they assume. But nothing could be further from the truth.

Design principle 4: Test products with as many stakeholders as possible

Companies would do well to map out the entire chain of stakeholders who will determine a product's success, at the beginning of the design process. In addition to asking who the end user will be and what he or she needs, companies must consider who will make the product, distribute it, sell it, pay for it, repair it, and dispose of it. This will help in developing not just the product but also a scalable business model.

It's best to adopt the attitude that you're designing with, not for, stakeholders. If treated as equals, they're more likely to participate in the process and provide honest feedback. When you're designing a prosthetic limb, for instance, collaborate with amputees, the clinics that provide the prostheses, and the organizations that pay for them. If you're able-bodied, it doesn't matter how many doctoral degrees you've earned; you still don't know what it's like to live with a prosthetic device in a developing country.

The MIT team formed partnerships with wheelchair builders and users throughout the developing world. Those stakeholders, who provided insights on how to make the wheelchair better, easier to manufacture, more robust, and cheaper, came up with ideas for several features. The team gathered further feedback through field trials in East Africa, Guatemala, and India, conducted in conjunction with local wheelchair manufacturing and supply organizations. The tests had a huge impact, resulting in several design modifications.

Although the first prototype performed well on rough terrain in East Africa, it didn't do so well indoors. It was too wide to go through a standard doorway, which the MIT designers hadn't noticed, and it was 20 pounds heavier than rival products were. For the next iteration, tested in Guatemala, the engineers reduced the chair's width by shaping the seat closer to the user's hips, bringing the wheels closer to the frame, and using narrower tires. By conducting a structural analysis, optimizing the strength-to-weight ratio of the frame, and reducing materials wherever possible, the team also decreased the LFC's weight by 20 pounds. That version performed well indoors, but several users felt they might fall out when traversing rough terrain. So the team included foot, waist, and chest straps to secure the user to the seat in tests in India. Users rated the third version at par with conventional wheelchairs indoors and far superior outdoors.

No matter how thorough engineers are, users expose design flaws that only they can notice. For instance, of the seven major improvements users suggested, only eliminating the LFC's excess weight had been evident to the MIT team before the East African trial. It's critical to test prototypes in the field with potential users and design solutions with organizations that will disseminate the product. Remember, design is iterative; you can't get it right the first time, so be prepared to test many prototypes.

Trap 5: Refusing to believe that products designed for emerging markets could have global appeal

Western companies tend to assume that consumers in developed markets, who are brand-conscious and performance-sensitive, will never want products from emerging markets, even if their prices are lower. Executives also worry that even if those products did catch on, they could be dangerous, cannibalizing higher-priced, higher-margin offerings.

Design principle 5: Use emerging-market constraints to create global winners

Before designing solutions, companies should identify the inherent constraints that will operate on the new product or service—such as low average consumer income, poor infrastructure, and limited natural resources. This list will dictate the requirements—like price, durability, and materials—that new designs must meet.

The constraints of developing countries usually force technological breakthroughs that help innovations crack global markets. The new products become platforms on which companies can add features and capabilities that will delight many tiers of consumers across the world. One example is the Logan, a car Renault designed specifically for Eastern European customers, who are price-sensitive and demand value. Launched in Romania in 2004, the Logan cost only $6,500 but offered greater size and trunk space, higher ground clearance, and more reliability than rival products. To ensure a low price, Renault used fewer parts than usual in the vehicle and manufactured it in Romania, where labor costs are relatively low.

Two years later, Renault decided to make the Logan attractive to consumers in developed markets, by adding more safety features and greater cosmetic appeal, including metallic colors. In France it sold the Logan for as much as $9,400. In Germany sales of the Logan jumped from 6,000 units to 85,000 units over a three-year period. By 2013 sales in Western Europe had reached 430,000 units—a 19% increase over 2012. Thus, while the constraints in Eastern Europe forced Renault to create a new auto design, the result was a product that delivered high value at low cost to consumers in Western Europe as well.

Something similar is happening with the LFC: Wheelchair users in the United States and Europe have noticed the media buzz about the product and want to buy it. The MIT team worked with Continuum, a Boston-based design studio, to conduct a study of what a U.S. version of the LFC could look like. The designers also tested the LFC with potential customers in the West to identify features to add. The GRIT Freedom Chair, as the developed world model is called, was designed to fit into car trunks in the United States. It also has quick-release wheels that users can remove with one hand and is made from bicycle parts available in the United States.

Although commercial production of the Freedom Chair began only in May 2015, it's on its way to success in the developed world. The venture the MIT team founded to make the chairs, Global Research Innovation and Technology, was one of four startups that received a diamond award at MassChallenge, the world's largest startup competition, three years ago. In 2014, GRIT ran a Kickstarter campaign to launch the Freedom Chair, meeting its funding goal in only five days.

How the Principles Pay Off

Few companies have avoided the traps we've described as well as the global shaving products giant Gillette did when designing an offering for India. As recently as a decade ago, Gillette made most of its money in that country by catering to top-of-the-pyramid consumers with pricey products. In 2005, Procter & Gamble acquired Gillette and immediately saw an opportunity to expand market share in the country.

Prodded by its new parent, which had been in India since the early 1990s, Gillette decided to develop a product for the 400 million middle-income Indians who shave primarily with double-edge razors. It began by exploring consumer requirements. After mapping out the value chain, from steel suppliers to end users, a cross-functional team conducted ethnographic research, spending over 3,000 hours with 1,000 would-be consumers.

Gillette learned that the needs of Indian shavers differ from those of their developed world counterparts in four ways:

Affordability

The price would be a critical constraint, since Gillette's main competitor, the double-edge razor, costs just Re 1 (less than 2 cents).

Safety

Consumers in this market segment sit on the floor in the dark early-morning hours and, using a small amount of still water, wield a mirror in one hand and a razor in the other. Shaving often results in nicks and cuts, because double-edge razors don't have a protective layer between the blade and the skin.

Even so, when Gillette's product designers watched Indian men shaving, most of the men did not cut themselves. Their response was simple: "We are experts; we don't cut ourselves." However, the team concluded that shaving requires concentration; Indian shavers could not relax or talk during the process for fear of injuring themselves. Gillette had identified a latent need: Most shavers were keen to relieve the tension by using a safer razor and blade.

Ease of use

Indian men have heavier beards and thicker facial hair than most American men do, and shave less frequently, so they have to tackle longer hairs. They also like to use a lot of shaving cream. All of that leads their razors to clog up quickly. With little running water at their disposal, Indian men need razors that they can easily rinse.

Close shaves

Gillette rightly assumed that Indian men want close shaves, as men across the world do, but the difference is that they do not place a premium on time. They spend up to 30 minutes shaving, whereas U.S. men spend five to seven minutes.

To come up with a competitive product, Gillette had to relearn the science of shaving with a single blade. It found that multiple passes of a single-blade razor can achieve a close shave because of the viscoelastic nature of hair. As a blade cuts strands of hair, it also pulls them out a little from the skin. The hairs don't spring back at once; the follicles act like the mechanisms that close a screen door slowly. Because the hairs continue to protrude, the next pass of the blade can cut them a little shorter. And so on.

This process helped Gillette hit upon a valuable design freedom: It could use only a single blade in its new razor, which drastically lowered the production cost. The new razor would also need 80% fewer parts than other razors did, greatly reducing manufacturing complexity.

Gillette's engineers then had to figure out how to flatten the skin before cutting the hairs to ensure a close shave without injury. They also had to understand the mechanics of flushing out the razor by swishing it in a cup of water. Finally, they had to balance competing requirements: Small teeth at the cartridge's front were necessary to flatten the skin before it made contact with the blade, while the rear had to have an unobstructed pass-through to allow hair and shaving cream to wash out easily.

Rethinking the razor from the ground up, the Gillette team also designed a unique pivoting head. That helped the user maneuver around the curves of the face and neck, particularly under the chin—an area difficult to shave. Seeing that Indians gripped razors in numerous ways, Gillette created a bulging handle and textured it to prevent slippage.

Gillette didn't stop at designing a product specifically for India; it also built a new business model to support it. To reduce production and transportation costs, it manufactures the product at several locations. And because India's distribution infrastructure consists of millions of mom-and-pop retailers, the team designed packaging that consumers could easily spot in any store.

Over time the American company did well in this Indian segment—mainly because it didn't set out to make the cheapest razor; it strove to make a product with superior value at an ultralow cost. The Gillette Guard razor costs Rs 15 (around 25 cents)—3% as much as the company's Mach3 razor and 2% as much as its Fusion Power razor—and each refill blade costs Rs 5 (8 cents). Introduced in 2010, the innovative product has quickly gained market share: Two out of three razors sold in India today are Gillette Guards. Although

Gillette has not sold the Guard outside India yet, it embodies the promise of a successful reverse innovation.

———————

Though most Western companies know that the business world has changed dramatically in the past 15 years, they still don't realize that its center of gravity has pretty much shifted to emerging markets. China, India, Brazil, Russia, and Mexico are all likely to be among the world's 12 largest economies by 2030, and any company that wants to remain a market leader will have to focus on consumers there. Chief executives have no choice but to start investing in the infrastructure, processes, and people needed to develop products in emerging markets. Doing so will also allow multinationals to benefit from the "frugal engineering" (as Renault's CEO Carlos Ghosn labeled it) that's possible there. Because of abundant skilled talent—especially engineers—and relatively low salaries in those countries, the costs of creating products there are often lower than in developed nations. But no amount of investment will result in portfolios of successful new products and services if companies don't follow the design principles that govern the development of reverse innovations.

Originally published in July–August 2015. Reprint R1507F

Strategies for Learning from Failure

by Amy C. Edmondson

THE **WISDOM OF LEARNING** from failure is incontrovertible. Yet organizations that do it well are extraordinarily rare. This gap is not due to a lack of commitment to learning. Managers in the vast majority of enterprises that I have studied over the past 20 years—pharmaceutical, financial services, product design, telecommunications, and construction companies; hospitals; and NASA's space shuttle program, among others—genuinely wanted to help their organizations learn from failures to improve future performance. In some cases they and their teams had devoted many hours to after-action reviews, postmortems, and the like. But time after time I saw that these painstaking efforts led to no real change. The reason: Those managers were thinking about failure the wrong way.

Most executives I've talked to believe that failure is bad (of course!). They also believe that learning from it is pretty straightforward: Ask people to reflect on what they did wrong and exhort them to avoid similar mistakes in the future—or, better yet, assign a team to review and write a report on what happened and then distribute it throughout the organization.

These widely held beliefs are misguided. First, failure is not always bad. In organizational life it is sometimes bad, sometimes inevitable, and sometimes even good. Second, learning from organizational failures is anything but straightforward. The attitudes and activities required to effectively detect and analyze failures are in short supply in most companies, and the need for context-specific learning strategies is underappreciated. Organizations need new and better ways to go beyond lessons that are superficial ("Procedures weren't followed") or self-serving ("The market just wasn't ready for our great new product"). That means jettisoning old cultural beliefs and stereotypical notions of success and embracing failure's lessons. Leaders can begin by understanding how the blame game gets in the way.

The Blame Game

Failure and fault are virtually inseparable in most households, organizations, and cultures. Every child learns at some point that admitting failure means taking the blame. That is why so few organizations have shifted to a culture of psychological safety in which the rewards of learning from failure can be fully realized.

Executives I've interviewed in organizations as different as hospitals and investment banks admit to being torn: How can they respond constructively to failures without giving rise to an anything-goes attitude? If people aren't blamed for failures, what will ensure that they try as hard as possible to do their best work?

This concern is based on a false dichotomy. In actuality, a culture that makes it safe to admit and report on failure can—and in some organizational contexts *must*—coexist with high standards for performance. To understand why, look at the exhibit "A Spectrum of Reasons for Failure," which lists causes ranging from deliberate deviation to thoughtful experimentation.

Which of these causes involve blameworthy actions? Deliberate deviance, first on the list, obviously warrants blame. But inattention might not. If it results from a lack of effort, perhaps it's blameworthy. But if it results from fatigue near the end of an overly long shift, the manager who assigned the shift is more at fault than the employee. As we go down the list, it gets more and more difficult to find blameworthy acts. In fact, a failure resulting from thoughtful

STRATEGIES FOR LEARNING FROM FAILURE

Idea in Brief

The ingrained attitude that all failures are bad means organizations don't learn from them.

Leaders need to recognize that failures occur on a spectrum from blameworthy to praiseworthy, and that they fall into three categories:

- Failures in routine or predictable operations, which can be prevented

- Those in complex operations, which can't be avoided but can be managed so that they don't mushroom into catastrophes

- Unwanted outcomes in, for example, research settings, which are valuable because they generate knowledge

Although learning from failures requires different strategies in different work settings, the goal should be to detect them early, analyze them deeply, and design experiments or pilot projects to produce them. But if the organization is ultimately to succeed, employees must feel safe admitting to and reporting failures. Creating that environment takes strong leadership.

experimentation that generates valuable information may actually be praiseworthy.

When I ask executives to consider this spectrum and then to estimate how many of the failures in their organizations are truly blameworthy, their answers are usually in single digits—perhaps 2% to 5%. But when I ask how many are *treated* as blameworthy, they say (after a pause or a laugh) 70% to 90%. The unfortunate consequence is that many failures go unreported and their lessons are lost.

Not All Failures Are Created Equal

A sophisticated understanding of failure's causes and contexts will help to avoid the blame game and institute an effective strategy for learning from failure. Although an infinite number of things can go wrong in organizations, mistakes fall into three broad categories: preventable, complexity-related, and intelligent.

Preventable failures in predictable operations

Most failures in this category can indeed be considered "bad." They usually involve deviations from spec in the closely defined processes of high-volume or routine operations in manufacturing

A Spectrum of Reasons for Failure

- **Deviance.** An individual chooses to violate a prescribed process or practice.

- **Inattention.** An individual inadvertently deviates from specifications.

- **Lack of ability.** An individual doesn't have the skills, conditions, or training to execute a job.

- **Process inadequacy.** A competent individual adheres to a prescribed but faulty or incomplete process.

- **Task challenge.** An individual faces a task too difficult to be executed reliably every time.

- **Process complexity.** A process composed of many elements breaks down when it encounters novel interactions.

- **Uncertainty.** A lack of clarity about future events causes people to take seemingly reasonable actions that produce undesired results.

- **Hypothesis testing.** An experiment conducted to prove that an idea or a design will succeed fails.

- **Exploratory testing.** An experiment conducted to expand knowledge and investigate a possibility leads to an undesired result.

and services. With proper training and support, employees can follow those processes consistently. When they don't, deviance, inattention, or lack of ability is usually the reason. But in such cases, the causes can be readily identified and solutions developed. Checklists (as in the Harvard surgeon Atul Gawande's recent bestseller *The Checklist Manifesto*) are one solution. Another is the vaunted Toyota Production System, which builds continual learning from tiny failures (small process deviations) into its approach to improvement. As most students of operations know well, a team member on a Toyota assembly line who spots a problem or even a potential problem is encouraged to pull a rope called the andon cord, which immediately initiates a diagnostic and problem-solving process. Production continues unimpeded if the problem can be remedied in less than a

minute. Otherwise, production is halted—despite the loss of revenue entailed—until the failure is understood and resolved.

Unavoidable failures in complex systems

A large number of organizational failures are due to the inherent
uncertainty of work: A particular combination of needs, people, and
problems may have never occurred before. Triaging patients in a
hospital emergency room, responding to enemy actions on the bat-
tlefield, and running a fast-growing startup all occur in unpredictable situations. And in complex organizations like aircraft carriers
and nuclear power plants, system failure is a perpetual risk.

Although serious failures can be averted by following best practices for safety and risk management, including a thorough analysis
of any such events that do occur, small process failures are inevitable.
To consider them bad is not just a misunderstanding of how complex
systems work; it is counterproductive. Avoiding consequential failures means rapidly identifying and correcting small failures. Most
accidents in hospitals result from a series of small failures that went
unnoticed and unfortunately lined up in just the wrong way.

Intelligent failures at the frontier

Failures in this category can rightly be considered "good," because
they provide valuable new knowledge that can help an organization leap ahead of the competition and ensure its future growth—
which is why the Duke University professor of management Sim
Sitkin calls them intelligent failures. They occur when experimentation is necessary: when answers are not knowable in advance
because this exact situation hasn't been encountered before and
perhaps never will be again. Discovering new drugs, creating a radically new business, designing an innovative product, and testing
customer reactions in a brand-new market are tasks that require
intelligent failures. "Trial and error" is a common term for the
kind of experimentation needed in these settings, but it is a mis-
nomer, because "error" implies that there was a "right" outcome
in the first place. At the frontier, the right kind of experimentation produces good failures quickly. Managers who practice it can

avoid the *unintelligent* failure of conducting experiments at a larger scale than necessary.

Leaders of the product design firm IDEO understood this when they launched a new innovation-strategy service. Rather than help clients design new products within their existing lines—a process IDEO had all but perfected—the service would help them create new lines that would take them in novel strategic directions. Knowing that it hadn't yet figured out how to deliver the service effectively, the company started a small project with a mattress company and didn't publicly announce the launch of a new business.

Although the project failed—the client did not change its product strategy—IDEO learned from it and figured out what had to be done differently. For instance, it hired team members with MBAs who could better help clients create new businesses and made some of the clients' managers part of the team. Today strategic innovation services account for more than a third of IDEO's revenues.

Tolerating unavoidable process failures in complex systems and intelligent failures at the frontiers of knowledge won't promote mediocrity. Indeed, tolerance is essential for any organization that wishes to extract the knowledge such failures provide. But failure is still inherently emotionally charged; getting an organization to accept it takes leadership.

Building a Learning Culture

Only leaders can create and reinforce a culture that counteracts the blame game and makes people feel both comfortable with and responsible for surfacing and learning from failures. (See the sidebar "How Leaders Can Build a Psychologically Safe Environment.") They should insist that their organizations develop a clear understanding of what happened—not of "who did it"—when things go wrong. This requires consistently reporting failures, small and large; systematically analyzing them; and proactively searching for opportunities to experiment.

Leaders should also send the right message about the nature of the work, such as reminding people in R&D, "We're in the discovery business, and the faster we fail, the faster we'll succeed." I have found that managers often don't understand or appreciate this subtle but crucial point. They also may approach failure in a way that is inappropriate for the context. For example, statistical process control, which uses data analysis to assess unwarranted variances, is not good for catching and correcting random invisible glitches such as software bugs. Nor does it help in the development of creative new products. Conversely, though great scientists intuitively adhere to IDEO's slogan, "Fail often in order to succeed sooner," it would hardly promote success in a manufacturing plant.

Often one context or one kind of work dominates the culture of an enterprise and shapes how it treats failure. For instance, automotive companies, with their predictable, high-volume operations, understandably tend to view failure as something that can and should be prevented. But most organizations engage in all three kinds of work discussed above—routine, complex, and frontier. Leaders must ensure that the right approach to learning from failure is applied in each. All organizations learn from failure through three essential activities: detection, analysis, and experimentation.

Detecting Failure

Spotting big, painful, expensive failures is easy. But in many organizations any failure that can be hidden *is* hidden as long as it's unlikely to cause immediate or obvious harm. The goal should be to surface it early, before it has mushroomed into disaster.

Shortly after arriving from Boeing to take the reins at Ford, in September 2006, Alan Mulally instituted a new system for detecting failures. He asked managers to color code their reports green for good, yellow for caution, or red for problems—a common management technique. According to a 2009 story in *Fortune*, at his first few meetings all the managers coded their operations green, to Mulally's frustration. Reminding them that the company had lost several billion dollars the previous year, he asked straight out, "Isn't anything *not* going well?" After one tentative yellow report was made about a serious product defect that would probably delay a launch, Mulally

How Leaders Can Build a Psychologically Safe Environment

IF AN ORGANIZATION'S EMPLOYEES ARE to help spot existing and pending failures and to learn from them, their leaders must make it safe to speak up. Julie Morath, the chief operating officer of Children's Hospital and Clinics of Minnesota from 1999 to 2009, did just that when she led a highly successful effort to reduce medical errors. Here are five practices I've identified in my research, with examples of how Morath employed them to build a psychologically safe environment.

Frame the Work Accurately

People need a shared understanding of the kinds of failures that can be expected to occur in a given work context (routine production, complex operations, or innovation) and why openness and collaboration are important for surfacing and learning from them. Accurate framing detoxifies failure.

In a complex operation like a hospital, many consequential failures are the result of a series of small events. To heighten awareness of this system complexity, Morath presented data on U.S. medical error rates, organized discussion groups, and built a team of key influencers from throughout the organization to help spread knowledge and understanding of the challenge.

Embrace Messengers

Those who come forward with bad news, questions, concerns, or mistakes should be rewarded rather than shot. Celebrate the value of the news first and then figure out how to fix the failure and learn from it.

Morath implemented "Blameless Reporting"—an approach that encouraged employees to reveal medical errors and near misses anonymously. Her team created a new patient safety report, which expanded on the previous version by asking employees to describe incidents in their own words and to comment on the possible causes. Soon after the new system was implemented, the rate of reported failures shot up. Morath encouraged her people to view the data as good news, because the hospital could learn from failures—and made sure that teams were assigned to analyze every incident.

Acknowledge Limits

Being open about what you don't know, mistakes you've made, and what you can't get done alone will encourage others to do the same.

As soon as she joined the hospital, Morath explained her passion for patient safety and acknowledged that as a newcomer, she had only limited knowledge of how things worked at Children's. In group presentations and one-on-one discussions, she made clear that she would need everyone's help to reduce errors.

Invite Participation

Ask for observations and ideas and create opportunities for people to detect and analyze failures and promote intelligent experiments. Inviting participation helps defuse resistance and defensiveness.

Morath set up cross-disciplinary teams to analyze failures and personally asked thoughtful questions of employees at all levels. Early on, she invited people to reflect on their recent experiences in caring for patients: Was everything as safe as they would have wanted it to be? This helped them recognize that the hospital had room for improvement. Suddenly, people were lining up to help.

Set Boundaries and Hold People Accountable

Paradoxically, people feel psychologically safer when leaders are clear about what acts are blameworthy. And there must be consequences. But if someone is punished or fired, tell those directly and indirectly affected what happened and why it warranted blame.

When she instituted blameless reporting, Morath explained to employees that although reporting would not be punished, specific behaviors (such as reckless conduct, conscious violation of standards, failing to ask for help when over one's head) would. If someone makes the same mistake three times and is then laid off, coworkers usually express relief, along with sadness and concern—they understand that patients were at risk and that extra vigilance was required from others to counterbalance the person's shortcomings.

responded to the deathly silence that ensued with applause. After that, the weekly staff meetings were full of color.

That story illustrates a pervasive and fundamental problem: Although many methods of surfacing current and pending failures exist, they are grossly underutilized. Total Quality Management and soliciting feedback from customers are well-known techniques for bringing to light failures in routine operations. High-reliability-organization (HRO) practices help prevent catastrophic failures in complex systems like nuclear power plants through early detection. Électricité de France, which operates 58 nuclear power plants, has been an exemplar in this area: It goes beyond regulatory requirements and religiously tracks each plant for anything even slightly out of the ordinary, immediately investigates whatever turns up, and informs all its other plants of any anomalies.

Such methods are not more widely employed because all too many messengers—even the most senior executives—remain reluctant to convey bad news to bosses and colleagues. One senior executive I know in a large consumer products company had grave reservations about a takeover that was already in the works when he joined the management team. But, overly conscious of his newcomer status, he was silent during discussions in which all the other executives seemed enthusiastic about the plan. Many months later, when the takeover had clearly failed, the team gathered to review what had happened. Aided by a consultant, each executive considered what he or she might have done to contribute to the failure. The newcomer, openly apologetic about his past silence, explained that others' enthusiasm had made him unwilling to be "the skunk at the picnic."

In researching errors and other failures in hospitals, I discovered substantial differences across patient-care units in nurses' willingness to speak up about them. It turned out that the behavior of mid-level managers—how they responded to failures and whether they encouraged open discussion of them, welcomed questions, and displayed humility and curiosity—was the cause. I have seen the same pattern in a wide range of organizations.

A horrific case in point, which I studied for more than two years, is the 2003 explosion of the *Columbia* space shuttle, which killed seven astronauts (see "Facing Ambiguous Threats," by Michael A. Roberto, Richard M.J. Bohmer, and Amy C. Edmondson, HBR, November 2006). NASA managers spent some two weeks downplaying the seriousness of a piece of foam's having broken off the left side of the shuttle at launch. They rejected engineers' requests to resolve the ambiguity (which could have been done by having a satellite photograph the shuttle or asking the astronauts to conduct a space walk to inspect the area in question), and the major failure went largely undetected until its fatal consequences 16 days later. Ironically, a shared but unsubstantiated belief among program managers that there was little they could do contributed to their inability to detect the failure. Postevent analyses suggested that they might indeed have taken fruitful action. But clearly leaders hadn't established the necessary culture, systems, and procedures.

One challenge is teaching people in an organization when to declare defeat in an experimental course of action. The human tendency to hope for the best and try to avoid failure at all costs gets in the way, and organizational hierarchies exacerbate it. As a result, failing R&D projects are often kept going much longer than is scientifically rational or economically prudent. We throw good money after bad, praying that we'll pull a rabbit out of a hat. Intuition may tell engineers or scientists that a project has fatal flaws, but the formal decision to call it a failure may be delayed for months.

Again, the remedy—which does not necessarily involve much time and expense—is to reduce the stigma of failure. Eli Lilly has done this since the early 1990s by holding "failure parties" to honor intelligent, high-quality scientific experiments that fail to achieve the desired results. The parties don't cost much, and redeploying valuable resources—particularly scientists—to new projects earlier rather than later can save hundreds of thousands of dollars, not to mention kickstart potential new discoveries.

Analyzing Failure

Once a failure has been detected, it's essential to go beyond the obvious and superficial reasons for it to understand the root causes. This requires the discipline—better yet, the enthusiasm—to use sophisticated analysis to ensure that the right lessons are learned and the right remedies are employed. The job of leaders is to see that their organizations don't just move on after a failure but stop to dig in and discover the wisdom contained in it.

Why is failure analysis often shortchanged? Because examining our failures in depth is emotionally unpleasant and can chip away at our self-esteem. Left to our own devices, most of us will speed through or avoid failure analysis altogether. Another reason is that analyzing organizational failures requires inquiry and openness, patience, and a tolerance for causal ambiguity. Yet managers typically admire and are rewarded for decisiveness, efficiency, and action—not thoughtful reflection. That is why the right culture is so important.

The challenge is more than emotional; it's cognitive, too. Even without meaning to, we all favor evidence that supports our existing beliefs rather than alternative explanations. We also tend to downplay our responsibility and place undue blame on external or situational factors when we fail, only to do the reverse when assessing the failures of others—a psychological trap known as *fundamental attribution error*.

My research has shown that failure analysis is often limited and ineffective—even in complex organizations like hospitals, where human lives are at stake. Few hospitals systematically analyze medical errors or process flaws in order to capture failure's lessons. Recent research in North Carolina hospitals, published in November 2010 in the *New England Journal of Medicine*, found that despite a dozen years of heightened awareness that medical errors result in thousands of deaths each year, hospitals have not become safer.

Fortunately, there are shining exceptions to this pattern, which continue to provide hope that organizational learning is possible. At Intermountain Healthcare, a system of 23 hospitals that serves Utah and southeastern Idaho, physicians' deviations from medical protocols are routinely analyzed for opportunities to improve the

Designing Successful Failures

PERHAPS UNSURPRISINGLY, PILOT PROJECTS are usually designed to succeed rather than to produce intelligent failures—those that generate valuable information. To know if you've designed a genuinely useful pilot, consider whether your managers can answer yes to the following questions:

- Is the pilot being tested under typical circumstances (rather than optimal conditions)?

- Do the employees, customers, and resources represent the firm's real operating environment?

- Is the goal of the pilot to learn as much as possible (rather than to demonstrate the value of the proposed offering)?

- Is the goal of learning well understood by all employees and managers?

- Is it clear that compensation and performance reviews are not based on a successful outcome for the pilot?

- Were explicit changes made as a result of the pilot test?

---

protocols. Allowing deviations and sharing the data on whether they actually produce a better outcome encourages physicians to buy into this program. (See "Fixing Health Care on the Front Lines," by Richard M.J. Bohmer, HBR, April 2010.)

Motivating people to go beyond first-order reasons (procedures weren't followed) to understanding the second- and third-order reasons can be a major challenge. One way to do this is to use interdisciplinary teams with diverse skills and perspectives. Complex failures in particular are the result of multiple events that occurred in different departments or disciplines or at different levels of the organization. Understanding what happened and how to prevent it from happening again requires detailed, team-based discussion and analysis.

A team of leading physicists, engineers, aviation experts, naval leaders, and even astronauts devoted months to an analysis of the *Columbia* disaster. They conclusively established not only the first-order cause—a piece of foam had hit the shuttle's leading edge during launch—but also second-order causes: A rigid hierarchy and schedule-obsessed culture at NASA made it especially difficult for engineers to speak up about anything but the most rock-solid concerns.

Promoting Experimentation

The third critical activity for effective learning is strategically producing failures—in the right places, at the right times—through systematic experimentation. Researchers in basic science know that although the experiments they conduct will occasionally result in a spectacular success, a large percentage of them (70% or higher in some fields) will fail. How do these people get out of bed in the morning? First, they know that failure is not optional in their work; it's part of being at the leading edge of scientific discovery. Second, far more than most of us, they understand that every failure conveys valuable information, and they're eager to get it before the competition does.

In contrast, managers in charge of piloting a new product or service—a classic example of experimentation in business—typically do whatever they can to make sure that the pilot is perfect right out of the starting gate. Ironically, this hunger to succeed can later inhibit the success of the official launch. Too often, managers in charge of pilots design optimal conditions rather than representative ones. Thus the pilot doesn't produce knowledge about what *won't* work.

In the very early days of DSL, a major telecommunications company I'll call Telco did a full-scale launch of that high-speed technology to consumer households in a major urban market. It was an unmitigated customer-service disaster. The company missed 75% of its commitments and found itself confronted with a staggering 12,000 late orders. Customers were frustrated and upset, and service reps couldn't even begin to answer all their calls. Employee morale suffered. How could this happen to a leading company with high satisfaction ratings and a brand that had long stood for excellence?

A small and extremely successful suburban pilot had lulled Telco executives into a misguided confidence. The problem was that the pilot did not resemble real service conditions: It was staffed with unusually personable, expert service reps and took place in a community of educated, tech-savvy customers. But DSL was a brand-new technology and, unlike traditional telephony, had to interface with customers' highly variable home computers and technical skills. This added complexity and unpredictability to the service-delivery challenge in ways that Telco had not fully appreciated before the launch.

A more useful pilot at Telco would have tested the technology with limited support, unsophisticated customers, and old computers. It would have been designed to discover everything that could go wrong—instead of proving that under the best of conditions everything would go right. (See the sidebar "Designing Successful Failures.") Of course, the managers in charge would have to have understood that they were going to be rewarded not for success but, rather, for producing intelligent failures as quickly as possible.

In short, exceptional organizations are those that go beyond detecting and analyzing failures and try to generate intelligent ones for the express purpose of learning and innovating. It's not that managers in these organizations enjoy failure. But they recognize it as a necessary by-product of experimentation. They also realize that they don't have to do dramatic experiments with large budgets. Often a small pilot, a dry run of a new technique, or a simulation will suffice.

The courage to confront our own and others' imperfections is crucial to solving the apparent contradiction of wanting neither to discourage the reporting of problems nor to create an environment in which anything goes. This means that managers must ask employees to be brave and speak up—and must not respond by expressing anger or strong disapproval of what may at first appear to be incompetence. More often than we realize, complex systems are at work behind organizational failures, and their lessons and improvement opportunities are lost when conversation is stifled.

Savvy managers understand the risks of unbridled toughness. They know that their ability to find out about and help resolve problems depends on their ability to learn about them. But most managers I've encountered in my research, teaching, and consulting work are far more sensitive to a different risk—that an understanding response to failures will simply create a lax work environment in which mistakes multiply.

This common worry should be replaced by a new paradigm—one that recognizes the inevitability of failure in today's complex work organizations. Those that catch, correct, and learn from failure before others do will succeed. Those that wallow in the blame game will not.

Originally published in April 2011. Reprint R1104B

How Indra Nooyi Turned Design Thinking into Strategy

An interview with Indra Nooyi. *by Adi Ignatius*

JUST A FEW YEARS AGO, it wasn't clear whether Indra Nooyi would survive as PepsiCo's CEO. Many investors saw Pepsi as a bloated giant whose top brands were losing market share. And they were critical of Nooyi's shift toward a more health-oriented overall product line. Prominent activist investor Nelson Peltz fought hard to split the company in two.

These days Nooyi, 59, exudes confidence. The company has enjoyed steady revenue growth during her nine years in the top job, and Pepsi's stock price is rising again after several flat years. Peltz even agreed to a truce in return for a board seat for one of his allies.

All of this frees Nooyi to focus on what she says is now driving innovation in the company: design thinking. In 2012 she brought in Mauro Porcini as Pepsi's first-ever chief design officer. Now, Nooyi says, "design" has a voice in nearly every important decision that the company makes.

To understand Pepsi's transformation, I spoke with Nooyi at the company's temporary headquarters in White Plains, New York (the real one, in Purchase, is being renovated). She talked about what design means to her, the challenges in changing a culture, and her proudest achievement.

—*Adi Ignatius*

HBR: *What problem were you trying to solve by making PepsiCo more design-driven?*

Nooyi: As CEO, I visit a market every week to see what we look like on the shelves. I always ask myself—not as a CEO but as a mom—"What products really speak to me?" The shelves just seem more and more cluttered, so I thought we had to rethink our innovation process and design experiences for our consumers—from conception to what's on the shelf.

How did you begin to drive that change?

First, I gave each of my direct reports an empty photo album and a camera. I asked them to take pictures of anything they thought represented good design.

What did you get back from them?

After six weeks, only a few people returned the albums. Some had their wives take pictures. Many did nothing at all. They didn't know what design was. Every time I tried to talk about design within the company, people would refer to packaging: "Should we go to a different blue?" It was like putting lipstick on a pig, as opposed to redesigning the pig itself. I realized we needed to bring a designer into the company.

How easy was it to find Mauro Porcini?

We did a search, and we saw that he'd achieved this kind of success at 3M. So we brought him in to talk about our vision. He said he wanted resources, a design studio, and a seat at the table. We gave him all of that. Now our teams are pushing design

Idea in Brief

CEO Indra Nooyi believes that each PepsiCo product must engage customers so directly and personally that they fall in love with it. So in 2012 she hired renowned designer Mauro Porcini as PepsiCo's first chief design officer. Nooyi says that design thinking now informs nearly everything the company does, from product creation, to the look on the shelf, to how consumers interact with a product *after* they buy it.

Design thinking is apparent, for instance, in Pepsi Spire, the company's touchscreen fountain machine that gives consumers the visual experience of watching flavors get added to a beverage before the finished product is

dispensed. And design thinking is an integral part of what Nooyi says makes women embrace Mountain Dew Kickstart—with its slim can, higher juice content, and lower calorie burden—as a product they can "walk around with."

But design is not all about the way a product looks, according to Nooyi. She says that PepsiCo has delivered "great shareholder value" on her watch because the company also offers consumers true choices, as evident in its "good for you" and "fun for you" categories of products—and because she has led her workforce to adapt strategically to consumers' constantly evolving aspirations.

through the entire system, from product creation, to packaging and labeling, to how a product looks on the shelf, to how consumers interact with it.

What's your definition of good design?

For me, a well-designed product is one you fall in love with. Or you hate. It may be polarizing, but it has to provoke a real reaction. Ideally, it's a product you want to engage with in the future, rather than just "Yeah, I bought it, and I ate it."

You say it's not just about packaging, but a lot of what you're talking about seems to be that.

It's much more than packaging. We had to rethink the entire experience, from conception to what's on the shelf to the postproduct experience. Let's take Pepsi Spire, our new touchscreen fountain machine. Other companies with dispensing machines have focused on adding a few more buttons and combinations of flavors. Our design guys essentially said that we're talking about a fundamentally different interaction between consumer and machine. We basically have a gigantic iPad on a futuristic machine that talks to you and invites you to interact with it. It tracks what you buy so that in the future, when you swipe your ID, it reminds you of the flavor combinations you tried last time and suggests new ones. It displays beautiful shots of the product, so when you add lime or cranberry, it actually shows those flavors being added—you *experience* the infusion of the flavor, as opposed to merely hitting a button and out comes the finished product.

Have you developed other notable design-led innovations?

We're working on new products for women. Our old approach was "shrink it or pink it." We'd put Doritos, say, in a pink Susan G. Komen bag and say it's for women. That's fine, but there's more to how women like to snack.

OK, how do women like to snack?

When men finish a snack bag, they pour what's left into their mouths. Women don't do that. And they worry about how much the product may stain—they won't rub it on a chair, which a lot of guys do. In China, we've introduced a stacked chip that comes in a plastic tray inside a canister. When a woman wants to snack, she can open her drawer and eat from the tray. When she's done, she can push it back in. The chip is also less noisy to eat: Women don't want people to hear them crunching away.

Basically, you're paying a lot more attention to user experience.

Definitely. In the past, user experience wasn't part of our lexicon. Focusing on crunch, taste, and everything else now pushes us to rethink shape, packaging, form, and function. All of that has consequences for what machinery we put in place—to produce, say, a plastic tray instead of a flex bag. We're forcing the design thinking way back in the supply chain.

To what extent do you listen to consumers? Do they even know what they want?

I don't know if consumers know what they want. But we can learn from them. Let's take SunChips. The original size was one inch by one inch. When you'd bite into a chip, it would break into pieces. In focus groups consumers told us they went to another product because it was bite-size. We had to conclude that SunChips were too damn big. I don't care if our mold can only cut one inch by one inch. We don't sell products based on the manufacturing we have, but on how our target consumers can fall in love with them.

Launch and Failure

When I picture design thinking, I think about rapid prototyping and testing. Is that part of what you're trying to do?

Not so much in the U.S., but China and Japan are lead horses for that process—test, prove, launch. If you launch quickly, you have more failures, but that's OK because the cost of failure in those markets is low. In the U.S., we tend to follow very organized processes and then launch. The China-Japan model may have to come to the United States at some point.

Isn't this model already established in the U.S., or at least in Silicon Valley?

Lots of small companies take this approach, and for them the cost of failure is acceptable. We're more cautious, especially when playing with big brands. Line extensions are fine: If you launch a flavor of Doritos that doesn't work, you just pull it. But if you launch a new product, you want to make sure you've tested it enough. In Japan, we launch a new version of Pepsi every three months—green, pink, blue. We just launched cucumber-flavored Pepsi. In three months it either works or we pull it and go to the next product.

Is your design approach giving Pepsi competitive advantage?

We have to do two things as a company: Keep our top line growing in the mid single digits, and grow our bottom line faster than the top. Line extensions keep the base growing. And then we're always looking for hero products—the two or three big products that will drive the top line significantly in a particular country or segment. Mountain Dew Kickstart is one of those. It's a completely different product: higher juice content, fewer calories, new flavors. We thought about this innovation differently. In the past we just would have created new flavors of Mountain Dew. But Kickstart comes in a slim can and doesn't look or taste like the old Mountain Dew. It's bringing new users into the franchise: women who say, "Hey, this is an 80-calorie product with juice in a package I can walk around with." It has generated more than $200 million in two years, which in our business is hard to do.

Is this an example of design thinking, or just part of the innovation process?
There's a fine line between innovation and design. Ideally, design leads to innovation and innovation demands design. We're just getting started. Innovation accounted for 9% of our net revenue last year. I'd like to raise that to the mid teens, because I think the marketplace is getting more creative. To get there, we'll have to be willing to tolerate more failure and shorter cycles of adaptation.

Do you feel that companies have to reinvent themselves every few years, that competitive advantage is fleeting?
No question about it. It's been a long time since you could talk about sustainable competitive advantage. The cycles are shortened. The rule used to be that you'd reinvent yourself once every seven to 10 years. Now it's every two to three years. There's constant reinvention: how you do business, how you deal with the customer.

Managing Change

How do you bring everyone in the company along with what sounds like a dramatic change in approach?
The most important thing was finding the right person in Mauro. Our beverage people immediately embraced how he could help us

think about product design and development. Then retailers fell in love with him and started inviting him to their shops to talk about how to reset their shelves. Mauro's team grew from about 10 people to almost 50, and we set him up in SoHo in New York City. Now our products look like they're tailored to the right cohort groups, and our packaging looks pretty damn good, too.

How do you push the culture change throughout the company?

In the past, being decentralized was our strength, but also our weakness. It's a fine approach when the whole world is growing and life is peachy. But it doesn't work when things are volatile globally and you need coordination. We've given our people 24 to 36 months to adapt. I told everyone that if they don't change, I'd be happy to attend their retirement parties.

How do you measure whether or not people are making it?

We watch how they act in our global meetings and whether they include design early in the process. We see how much innovation, influenced by design, is being put into the market. We maintain an aggressive productivity program to take costs out and free up resources. You have to squeeze as much as you can out of every dollar, and we watch how many costs are coming out.

Purpose and the Portfolio

You often use the term "purpose" in talking about your business. What does that mean to you?

When I became CEO in 2006, I did a series of town hall meetings with employees. Few said they came to work for a paycheck. Most wanted to build a life, not simply gain a livelihood. And they were well aware that consumers cared about health and wellness. We realized we needed to engage our people's heads, hearts, and hands. We had to produce more products that are good for you. We had to embrace sustainability. Purpose is not about giving money away for social responsibility. It's about fundamentally changing how to make money in order to deliver performance—to help ensure that PepsiCo is a "good" company where young people want to work.

Would you be willing to accept lower profit margins to "do the right thing"? Surely, there have to be trade-offs.

Purpose doesn't hurt margins. Purpose is how you drive transformation. If you don't transform the portfolio, you're going to stop top-line growth, and margins will decline anyway. So we don't really invest in "purpose," but in a strategy to keep the company successful in the future. If we hadn't tackled certain environmental issues, especially with water, we would have lost our licenses in some countries. Now, sometimes when you're changing the culture radically, you run into problems. Transformations sometimes hit your margins or top line because things don't always go in a straight line. But if you think in terms of the life span of the company, these are just small blips.

But aren't you still selling a lot of unhealthy products?

We make a portfolio of products, some of which are "fun for you" and some of which are "good for you." We sell sugary beverages and chips, but we also have Quaker Oats, Tropicana, Naked Juice, and Izze. We're reducing the salt, sugar, and fat in the core products. And we've dialed up the good-for-you offerings because societal needs have changed.

Would you consider stopping a popular product line because it doesn't meet the good-for-you standard?

That wouldn't make sense, because none of our products is bad or unsafe. We give consumers choices that reflect their lifestyles. If you want to consume Pepsi, we'll give you Pepsi in every size possible so that on one occasion you can consume 12 ounces and on another only seven and a half. We want to make sure that both the good-for-you and the fun-for-you products are readily available, affordably priced, and great tasting. And we make sure that good-for-you tastes as good as fun-for-you. We want you to love our Quaker Oats Real Medleys as much as you love Doritos Loaded.

Do you try to push sales of the healthier products?

Yes, but we also want to preserve choice. We've taken lessons from Richard Thaler and Cass Sunstein's book *Nudge*. We try to put portion-control packages out front on the shelves. We make sure our diet products are merchandised as aspirationally as our full-sugar products are. We advertise Gatorade only with athletes in mind because it's not intended to be a recreational beverage.

Consumers seem very demanding these days. How do you keep up with that?

We have to make sure we're engineering our portfolio for the consumer of the future. There's nothing wrong, for example, with aspartame. But if consumers say they don't like it, we have to give them a choice. We'll offer a diet product that's aspartame-free. Similarly, there's nothing wrong with high-fructose corn syrup, but if consumers say they like real sugar, we have to offer that, too.

What's your proudest accomplishment since becoming CEO?

I took over PepsiCo just after it had a string of successful years. Then everything changed. We faced new regulatory pressures on our fun-for-you categories, and our good-for-you business wasn't fully developed. The North American market slowed down, and we weren't big enough internationally. Sales through some major U.S. customers slowed down massively. Our key beverage competitor had done a big reset of its own, and it bounced back. We looked at ourselves and saw a decentralized, far-flung company that had to be knitted together. The culture needed to change. We had to eliminate redundancies. We had to slim down to reinvest in R&D, advertising and marketing, and new capabilities. I had a choice. I could have gone pedal to the metal, stripped out costs, delivered strong profit for a few years, and then said adios. But that wouldn't have yielded long-term success. So I articulated a strategy to the board focusing on the portfolio we needed to build, the muscles we needed to strengthen, the capabilities to develop. The board said, "We know there will be hiccups along the way, but you have our support, so go make it happen." We started to implement that strategy, and we've

---

PepsiCo's billion-dollar brands

Beverages	Food
Pepsi	Lay's
Mountain Dew	Doritos
Gatorade	Quaker
Tropicana	Cheetos
Diet Pepsi	Ruffles
7UP	Tostitos
Mirinda	Fritos
Lipton	Walkers Crisps
Aquafina	
Pepsi Max	
Brisk	
Sierra Mist	
Diet Mountain Dew	
Starbucks ready-to-drink beverages	

Source: PepsiCo FY14 annual report

---

delivered great shareholder value while strengthening the company for the long term.

Growing up in Madras, you seem to have broken every possible stereotypical expectation of a young girl in India. Are you still that person?

To a certain extent. When you're a CEO, you can't break too many stereotypical expectations. I wish you could, but you can't. In those days, there was a well-defined conservative stereotype, so everything I did was breaking the framework. I played in a rock band. I climbed trees. I did stuff that made my parents wonder, "What the hell is she doing?" But I also was a good student and a good daughter, so I never brought shame on the family. And I was lucky that the men in my family thought the women should have an equal shot at everything. I'm still a bit of a rebel, always saying that we cannot sit still. Every morning you've got to wake up with a healthy fear that the world is changing, and a conviction that, to win, you have to change faster and be more agile than anyone else.

Originally published in September 2015. Reprint R1509F

Spotlight

PepsiCo's Chief Design Officer on Creating an Organization Where Design Can Thrive

by James de Vries

Mauro Porcini is PepsiCo's chief design officer—the first to hold the position—where he oversees design-led innovation across all the company's brands under CEO Indra Nooyi. Below is an edited version of my conversation with Porcini on a variety of topics, from prototyping to the essential qualities of a great design organization.

How do you define design?

Design can mean many different things. At PepsiCo, we're leveraging design to create meaningful and relevant brand experiences for our customers any time they interact with our portfolio of products. Our work covers each brand's visual identity, from the product itself all the way to the marketing and merchandising activities that bring a brand to life across different platforms—music, sports, fashion, and so forth.

This applies not only to the current portfolio of products, but also to PepsiCo's future portfolio. That's where our work is really about

135

innovation. I strongly believe that design and innovation are exactly the same thing. Design is more than the aesthetics and artifacts associated with products; it's a strategic function that focuses on what people want and need and dream of, then crafts experiences across the full brand ecosystem that are meaningful and relevant for customers.

What does this look like on a day-to-day basis, at PepsiCo or elsewhere?

Design in this context relies on the prototyping process, which can create a lot of value inside organizations because it aligns the full organization around one idea. For instance, if I say "knife," you are going to visualize a kind of knife. I'm going to visualize another knife, and if there were other people in the room, they would visualize many different kinds of knives. But if I design a knife right now, I align everybody around that knife. Let's say that in the room there is a marketer who tells me the brand is not visible enough. There is an ergonomist who tells me the handle is not comfortable enough. There is a scientist who tells me the blade is not sharp enough. These are not mistakes. They're not failures in the process. They're how prototyping surfaces issues that don't emerge in the abstract. That's the power of design and prototyping.

When you put a prototype, something that is new and that nobody has ever seen before, in front of people, they get excited, right? There is the sparkle in the eye. I've seen it so many times in so many meetings. People talk and talk about things until somebody arrives with an object, a prototype, and then everybody gets excited. That's how you unlock resources. You unlock sponsorship engagement. That's extremely powerful and lets you move really fast. It's how you speed up your innovation process and make the outcome more relevant to customers.

What do you need in order to make design thrive inside an organization?

Certain circumstances are necessary for design to thrive in enterprises. First of all, you need to bring in the right kind of design leaders. That's where many organizations make mistakes.

If design is really about deeply understanding people and then strategizing around that, we need design leaders with broad skills.

Corporate executives often don't understand that there are different kinds of design: There is brand design. There is industrial design. There is interior design. There is UX and experience design. And there is innovation in strategy. So, you need a leader who can manage all the different phases of design in a very smart way—someone with a holistic vision.

Second, you need the right sponsorship from the top. The new design function and the new culture need to be protected by the CEO or by somebody at the executive level. Because any entity, any organization, tends to reject new culture.

Once you have that, then you need endorsements from a variety of different entities. It could be from other designers outside your organization. It could be from design magazines. It could be through awards. But you need that kind of external endorsement to validate for those inside the organization that you're moving in the right direction.

Then you need to identify quick wins: those projects where you can show the value of design very quickly inside the organization. On the basis of this early success, you start to build processes that can enable the new culture and approach to be integrated inside the organization.

The process is really an evolution. I see it as five often-overlapping phases. The first one is **denial**: the organization sees no need for a new approach or new culture. But somebody with influence and power inside the organization—often it's the CEO or somebody at executive level—understands that actually there is a need, so they hire a design leader who tries to introduce a new culture.

Then comes the second phase: **hidden rejection**. There may be acceptance at the top that the organization needs to embrace a new approach, but the full organization isn't there yet. The design leader is moving forward in alignment with leadership and thinks that things are working well, but in reality they are not. In this phase, it's easy to fail, and it's easy for the company to reject the new approach.

The third phase is what I call **the occasional leap of faith**. As the design leader, you find a coconspirator inside the organization who understands the value of what you're doing. He may or may not understand deeply what design is about, but he understands that there is value there and decides to build something with you, to bet on you. That's when you start to get your quick wins. The quick wins are so important because they exponentially build understanding about the value of design.

The fourth one is what I like to call **the quest for confidence**. This is when the company understands that there is value in this new design culture and tries to integrate it throughout the organization. The problem is that when you try to do something different, there is always inefficiency and risk. This is especially true if you do design in innovation: There is risk not just in a process but in the market, in the brand and product you're going to launch. That's when you need to build confidence in the organization.

But at the very base of innovation and entrepreneurship is risk. Methodologies like Six Sigma are all about reducing risk, but they are not effective for innovation because innovation by definition is risky. Design, on the other hand, can build confidence inside the organization in a variety of ways. It comes down to building innovation know-how within the organization, and gaining input and buy-in from across the organization and from your customer through the prototyping process. The more you prototype, the more you build confidence in the organization, and the more you know that what you're doing is the right thing. This quest for confidence is extremely important because so many corporations today are paralyzed by their fear of making mistakes or failing.

The last phase is what I like to call **holistic awareness**, when everybody understands that the new culture, in this case design, makes sense for the organization. This is when design is not about designers anymore. It becomes universal, and it prompts everybody to modify their own approach to work—whether it's marketing, manufacturing, or any other function—to embrace it.

What does a design team look like at PepsiCo?

You need the design function—senior leaders with teams under them—embedded inside the business organization. Or integrated into it, I should say, because we don't want design to report to another function. We want design to be a peer of marketing and to drive innovation.

At the center, we have been developing the key pillars of the design functions. We have a very senior leader running industrial design, another one running brand design, another one running innovation and strategy. And we are building digital as well. They are the ones who are nurturing the design capability.

Our hiring process is tough because we're not just looking for good designers. When you're creating a new design organization, a new culture, you need to hire change agents and people who understand how to change the culture of design. This makes things extremely difficult because you have many, many designers who may be *amazing* at what they do, but they have no idea how to explain what they are doing to a business organization. Those kinds of designers are a luxury we can't afford in this phase of the organization's evolution. If you have designers who can't influence change, you get that familiar situation with designers whining that the business organization doesn't understand them and the business organizations saying the design community has no clue what we're trying to do.

You need the shared language, the structure, and most of all the right people to create a true design culture. I'm really against those design or innovation firms that claim they can come in and teach you design thinking. The result of their expensive workshops is people who are not design experts will start to think that now they get design and can do it by themselves. That's a disaster because you do need skills and experience.

How do you convince others that investing in design is worth it?

For many, many years I've been asked in my corporate life to define the return on investment of design. The objective variables obviously are at project level and then at brand level—top-line and bottom-line growth. That's a no-brainer.

Then there are subjective variables that we really want to take into consideration. One is consumer engagement. You can measure it in a formal way or you can measure it in the way consumers talk about your products, which is easy to do today via social media. Another variable is brand equity, meaning the impact on the brand. It's customer engagement, the way your customers interact with you, the way they talk to you.

The truth is, once you embed design across your organization and people start to experience it, they stop asking you what its ROI is because they start to see the impact across all those variables.

Can you talk about a key business outcome from your time at PepsiCo so far?

When I joined the company a little less than three years ago, I was able to build a very strong partnership with our business organization and with R&D. We've been leveraging design to understand what our customers need and want from fountains, coolers, and vending machines. Then we've been crafting—prototyping, really—to create the ideal portfolio as fast as possible and take it to market.

The Spire family of equipment, launched about one year ago, is the first output of Pepsi's design-thinking approach. Spire is a series of fountains and vending machines that let you customize your drink: you choose the beverage and add flavors. It's been well received by the market, and it's helped us as a design organization to show what design is about. We launched a new series of products this year and there is much more in the pipeline, but Spire is probably the project I love the most.

What makes Spire significant is that it's such a change for the industry. Usually it's external partners and suppliers that do a lot of the work on equipment, but with Spire, we said, let's reset and let's try to understand what makes up the portfolio of products we really want to offer. We rethought the architecture of the existing machines, but we also reimagined how we might build beverage, and eventually food, experiences in restaurants in the future.

We actually projected further out, to the fountain and the vending machine of 20 years from now. We wanted to understand where we could go and then step back pragmatically to deliver innovation in the short term, the middle term, and then the longer term as well.

You need to prove the point of design through activity, actions, and projects—it's not just top-line and bottom-line returns. That will come. But it could be speed to market. It could be efficiency in the process. It could be employee engagement.

Are there any final thoughts you want to leave our readers with?

As designers—industrial designers, product designers, innovation designers—we are trained to understand all the different worlds of brand and business, R&D and technology, and especially people. We become experts of everything and experts of nothing. What we're really good at is speaking the languages of all the different worlds, then connecting those worlds to our design tools and to our ability to prototype and visualize ideas. When done well, design becomes a cultural interpreter and facilitator across the entire organization.

Originally published on hbr.org on August 11, 2015. Reprint HO29VL

.

Reclaim Your Creative Confidence

by Tom Kelley and David Kelley

MOST PEOPLE ARE BORN CREATIVE. As children, we revel in imaginary play, ask outlandish questions, draw blobs and call them dinosaurs. But over time, because of socialization and formal education, a lot of us start to stifle those impulses. We learn to be warier of judgment, more cautious, more analytical. The world seems to divide into "creatives" and "noncreatives," and too many people consciously or unconsciously resign themselves to the latter category.

And yet we know that creativity is essential to success in any discipline or industry. According to a recent IBM survey of chief executives around the world, it's the most sought-after trait in leaders today. No one can deny that creative thinking has enabled the rise and continued success of countless companies, from startups like Facebook and Google to stalwarts like Procter & Gamble and General Electric.

Students often come to Stanford University's "d.school" (which was founded by one of us—David Kelley—and is formally known as the Hasso Plattner Institute of Design) to develop their creativity. Clients work with IDEO, our design and innovation consultancy, for the same reason. But along the way, we've learned that our job isn't to *teach* them creativity. It's to help them *rediscover* their creative confidence—the natural ability to come up with new ideas and the courage to try them out. We do this by giving them strategies to get past four fears that hold most of us back: fear of the messy unknown, fear of being judged, fear of the first step, and fear of losing control.

Easier said than done, you might argue. But we know it's possible for people to overcome even their most deep-seated fears. Consider the work of Albert Bandura, a world-renowned psychologist and Stanford professor. In one series of early experiments, he helped people conquer lifelong snake phobias by guiding them through a series of increasingly demanding interactions. They would start by watching a snake through a two-way mirror. Once comfortable with that, they'd progress to observing it through an open door, then to watching someone else touch the snake, then to touching it themselves through a heavy leather glove, and, finally, in a few hours, to touching it with their own bare hands. Bandura calls this process of experiencing one small success after another "guided mastery." The people who went through it weren't just cured of a crippling fear they had assumed was untreatable. They also had less anxiety and more success in other parts of their lives, taking up new and potentially frightening activities like horseback riding and public speaking. They tried harder, persevered longer, and had more resilience in the face of failure. They had gained a new confidence in their ability to attain what they set out to do.

We've used much the same approach over the past 30 years to help people transcend the fears that block their creativity. You break challenges down into small steps and then build confidence by succeeding on one after another. Creativity is something you practice, not just a talent you're born with. The process may feel a little uncomfortable at first, but—as the snake phobics learned—the discomfort quickly fades away and is replaced with new confidence and capabilities.

Fear of the Messy Unknown

Creative thinking in business begins with having empathy for your customers (whether they're internal or external), and you can't get that sitting behind a desk. Yes, we know it's cozy in your office. Everything is reassuringly familiar; information comes

Idea in Brief

Most people are born creative. But over time, a lot of us learn to stifle those impulses. We become warier of judgment, more cautious, more analytical. The world seems to divide into "creatives" and "noncreatives," and too many people resign themselves to the latter category. And yet we know that creativity is essential to success in any discipline or industry.

The good news is that we all can rediscover our creative confidence. The trick is to overcome the four big fears that hold most of us back: fear of the messy unknown, fear of judgment, fear of the first step, and fear of losing control.

This chapter describes an approach based on the work of psychologist Albert Bandura in helping patients get over their snake phobias: You break challenges down into small steps and then build confidence by succeeding on one after another. Creativity is something you practice, not just a talent you are born with.

from predictable sources; contradictory data are weeded out and ignored. Out in the world, it's more chaotic. You have to deal with unexpected findings, with uncertainty, and with irrational people who say things you don't want to hear. But that is where you find insights—and creative breakthroughs. Venturing forth in pursuit of learning, even without a hypothesis, can open you up to new information and help you discover nonobvious needs. Otherwise, you risk simply reconfirming ideas you've already had or waiting for others—your customers, your boss, or even your competitors—to tell you what to do.

At the d.school, we routinely assign students to do this sort of anthropological fieldwork—to get out of their comfort zones and into the world—until, suddenly, they start doing it on their own. Consider a computer scientist, two engineers, and an MBA student, all of whom took the Extreme Affordability class taught by Stanford business school professor Jim Patell. They eventually realized that they couldn't complete their group project—to research and design a low-cost incubator for newborn babies in the developing world— while living in safe, suburban California. So they gathered their courage and visited rural Nepal. Talking with families and doctors firsthand, they learned that the babies in gravest danger were those

Tackling the Mess, One Step at a Time

by Caroline O'Connor and Sarah Stein Greenberg

You can work up the confidence to tackle the big fears that hold most of us back by starting small. Here are a few ways to get comfortable with venturing into the messy unknown. The list gets increasingly challenging, but you can follow the first two suggestions without even leaving your desk.

Lurk in Online Forums

Listen in as potential customers share information, air grievances, and ask questions—it's the virtual equivalent of hanging around a popular café. You're not looking for evaluations of features or cost; you're searching for clues about their concerns and desires.

Pick Up the Phone and Call Your Own Company's Customer Service Line

Walk through the experience as if you were a customer, noting how your problem is handled and how you're feeling along the way.

Seek Out an Unexpected Expert

What does the receptionist in your building know about your firm's customer experience? If you use a car service for work travel, what insights do the drivers have about your firm? If you're in health care, talk to a medical assistant, not a doctor. If you make a physical product, ask a repair person to tell you about common failure areas.

Act Like a Spy

Take a magazine and a pair of headphones to a store or an industry conference (or, if your customers are internal, a break room or lunch area). Pretend to read while you observe. Watch as if you were a kid, trying to understand what is going on. How are people interacting with your offering? What can you glean from their body language?

Casually Interview a Customer or Potential Customer

After you've gotten more comfortable venturing out, try this: Write down a few open-ended questions about your product or service. Go to a place where your customers tend to gather, find someone you'd be comfortable approaching, and say you'd like to ask a few questions. If the person refuses? No problem, just try someone else. Eventually you'll find someone who's dying to talk to you. Press for more detail with every question. Even if you think you understand, ask "Why is that?" or "Can you tell me more about that?" Get people to dig into their own underlying assumptions.

born prematurely in areas far from hospitals. Nepalese villagers didn't need a cheaper incubator at the hospital—they needed a fail-safe way to keep babies warm when they were away from doctors who could do so effectively. Those insights led the team to design a miniature "sleeping bag" with a pouch containing a special heat-storing wax. The Embrace Infant Warmer costs 99% less than a traditional incubator and can maintain the right temperature for up to six hours without an external power source. The innovation has the potential to save millions of low-birth-weight and premature babies every year, and it came about only because the team members were willing to throw themselves into unfamiliar territory.

Another example comes from two students, Akshay Kothari and Ankit Gupta, who took the d.school's Launchpad course. The class required them to start a company from scratch by the end of the 10-week academic quarter. Both were self-described "geeks"—technically brilliant, deeply analytical, and definitely shy. But they opted to work on their project—an elegant news reader for the then-newly released iPad—off-campus in a Palo Alto café where they'd be surrounded by potential users. Getting over the awkwardness of approaching strangers, Akshay gathered feedback by asking café patrons to experiment with his prototypes. Ankit coded hundreds of small variations to be tested each day—changing everything from interaction patterns to the size of a button. In a matter of weeks they rapidly iterated their way to a successful product. "We went from people saying, 'This is crap,'" says Akshay, "to 'Is this app preloaded on every iPad?'" The result—Pulse News—received public praise from Steve Jobs at a worldwide developer's conference only a few months later, has been downloaded by 15 million people, and is one of the original 50 apps in Apple's App Store Hall of Fame.

It's not just entrepreneurs and product developers who should get into "the mess." Senior managers also must hear directly from anyone affected by their decisions. For instance, midway through a management off-site IDEO held for ConAgra Foods, the executives broke away from their upscale conference rooms to explore gritty Detroit neighborhoods, where you can go miles without seeing a grocery store. They personally observed how inner-city residents reacted to food products and spoke with an urban farmer who hopes to turn abandoned lots into community gardens. Now, according to Al Bolles, ConAgra's executive vice president of research, quality, and innovation, such behavior is common at the company. "A few years ago, it was hard to pry my executive team away from the office," he says, "but now we venture out and get onto our customers' home turf to get insights about what they really need."

Fear of Being Judged

If the scribbling, singing, dancing kindergartner symbolizes unfettered creative expression, the awkward teenager represents the opposite: someone who cares—*deeply*—about what other people think. It takes only a few years to develop that fear of judgment, but it stays with us throughout our adult lives, often constraining our careers. Most of us accept that when we are learning, say, to ski, others will see us fall down until practice pays off. But we can't risk our business-world ego in the same way. As a result, we self-edit, killing potentially creative ideas because we're afraid our bosses or peers will see us fail. We stick to "safe" solutions or suggestions. We hang back, allowing others to take risks. But you can't be creative if you are constantly censoring yourself.

Half the battle is to resist judging *yourself*. If you can listen to your own intuition and embrace more of your ideas (good and bad), you're already partway to overcoming this fear. So take baby steps, as Bandura's clients did. Instead of letting thoughts run through your head and down the drain, capture them systematically in some form of idea notebook. Keep a whiteboard and marker in the shower. Schedule daily "white space" in your calendar, where your only task is to think or take a walk and daydream. When you try to generate ideas, shoot for 100 instead of 10. Defer your own judgment and you'll be surprised at how many ideas you have—and like—by the end of the week.

Also, try using new language when you give feedback, and encourage your collaborators to do the same. At the d.school, our feedback typically starts with "I like . . ." and moves on to "I wish . . ." instead of just passing judgment with put-downs like "That will never work." Opening with the positives and then using the first person for suggestions signals that "This is just my opinion and I want to help," which makes listeners more receptive to your ideas.

We recently worked with Air New Zealand to reinvent the customer experience for its long-distance flights. As a highly regulated industry, airlines tend toward conservatism. To overcome the cultural norm of skepticism and caution, we started with a workshop aimed at generating crazy ideas. Executives brainstormed and prototyped a dozen unconventional (and some seemingly impractical) concepts, including harnesses that hold people standing up, groups of seats facing one another around a table, and even hammocks and bunk beds. Everyone was doing it, so no one was scared he or she would be judged. This willingness to consider wild notions and defer judgment eventually led the Air New Zealand team to a creative breakthrough: the Skycouch, a lie-flat seat for economy class. At first, it seemed impossible that such a seat could be made without enlarging its footprint (seats in business and first-class cabins take up much more space), but the new design does just that: A heavily padded section swings up like a footrest to transform an airline row into a futon-like platform that a couple can lie down on together. The Skycouch is now featured on a number of Air New Zealand's international flights, and the company has won several industry awards as a result.

Fear of the First Step

Even when we want to embrace our creative ideas, acting on them presents its own challenges. Creative efforts are hardest at the beginning. The writer faces the blank page; the teacher, the start of school; businesspeople, the first day of a new project. In a broader sense, we're also talking about fear of charting a new path or breaking out of your predictable workflow. To overcome this inertia, good ideas are not enough. You need to stop planning and just get started—and the best way to do that is to stop focusing on the huge overall task and find a small piece you can tackle right away.

Bestselling writer Anne Lamott expertly captures this idea in a story from her childhood. Her brother had been assigned a school report about birds, but he waited to start on it until the night before it was due. He was near tears, overwhelmed by the task ahead, until his father gave him some wise advice: "Bird by bird, buddy. Just take it bird by bird." In a business context, you can push yourself to take the first step by asking: What is the low-cost experiment? What's the quickest, cheapest way to make progress toward the larger goal?

Or give yourself a crazy deadline, as John Keefe, a d.school alum and a senior editor at radio station WNYC, did after a colleague complained that her mom had to wait at city bus stops never knowing when the next bus would come. If you worked for New York City Transit and your boss asked you to solve that problem, how soon would you promise to get a system up and running? Six weeks? Ten? John, who *doesn't* work for the transit authority, said, "Give me till the end of the day." He bought an 800 number, figured out how to access real-time bus data, and linked it to text-to-speech technology. Within 24 hours, he had set up a service that allowed bus riders to call in, input their bus stop number, and hear the location of the approaching bus. John applies the same fearless attitude to his work at WNYC. "The most effective way I've found to practice design thinking is by showing, not telling," he explains.

Another example of the "start simple" strategy comes from an IDEO project to develop a new dashboard feature for a European luxury car. To test their ideas, designers videotaped an existing car and then used digital effects to layer on proposed features. The rapid prototyping process took less than a week. When the team showed the video to our client, he laughed. "Last time we did something like this," he said, "we built a prototype car, which took almost a year and cost over a million dollars. Then we took a video of it. You skipped the car and went straight to the video."

Our mantra is "Don't get ready, get started!" The first step will seem much less daunting if you make it a tiny one and you force yourself to do it *right now*. Rather than stalling and allowing your anxiety to build, just start inching toward the snake.

Fear of Losing Control

Confidence doesn't simply mean believing your ideas are good. It means having the humility to let go of ideas that aren't working and to accept good ideas from other people. When you abandon the status quo and work collaboratively, you sacrifice control over your product, your team, and your business. But the creative gains can more than compensate. Again, you can start small. If you're facing a tough challenge, try calling a meeting with people fresh to the topic. Or break the routine of a weekly meeting by letting the most junior person in the room set the agenda and lead it. Look for opportunities to cede control and leverage different perspectives.

That's exactly what Bonny Simi, director of airport planning at JetBlue Airways, did after an ice storm closed JFK International Airport for a six-hour stretch in 2007—and disrupted the airline's flight service for the next six days. Everyone knew there were operational problems to be fixed, but no one knew exactly what to do. Fresh from a d.school course, Bonny suggested that JetBlue brainstorm solutions from the bottom up rather than the top down. First, she gathered a team of 120 frontline employees together for just one day—pilots, flight attendants, dispatchers, ramp workers, crew schedulers, and other staff members. Then she mapped out their disruption recovery actions (using yellow Post-it notes) and the challenges they faced (using pink ones). By the end of the day, Bonny's grassroots task force had reached new insights—and resolve. The distributed team then spent the next few months working through more than a thousand pink Post-its to creatively solve each problem. By admitting that the answers lay in the collective, Bonny did more than she could ever have done alone. And JetBlue now recovers from major disruptions significantly faster than it did before.

Our own experience with the open innovation platform OpenIDEO is another case in point. Its launch was scary in two ways: First, we were starting a public conversation that could quickly get out of hand; second, we were admitting that we don't have all the answers. But we were ready, like Bandura's phobics, to take a bigger leap—to touch the snake. And we soon discovered the benefits. Today, the

OpenIDEO community includes about 30,000 people from 170 countries. They may never meet in person, but together they've already made a difference on dozens of initiatives—from helping revitalize cities in economic decline to prototyping ultrasound services for expectant mothers in Colombia. We've learned that no matter what group you're in or where you work, there are always more ideas outside than inside.

For people with backgrounds as diverse as those of Akshay, Ankit, John, and Bonny, fear—of the messy unknown, of judgment, of taking the first step, or of letting go—could have blocked the path to innovation. But instead, they worked to overcome their fears, rediscovered their creative confidence, and made a difference. As Hungarian essayist György Konrád once said, "Courage is only the accumulation of small steps." So don't wait at the starting line. Let go of your fears and begin practicing creative confidence today.

Originally published in December 2012. Reprint R1212K

About the Contributors

ROBERT D. AUSTIN is a professor of information systems and the faculty director of the Learning Innovation Initiative at Ivey Business School.

CHRISTIAN BASON is the CEO of the Danish Design Centre, a government-funded organization in Copenhagen.

TIM BROWN is Executive Chair of the international design consulting firm IDEO and the author of *Change by Design* (HarperBusiness, 2009).

CLAYTON M. CHRISTENSEN is the Kim B. Clark Professor at Harvard Business School and a coauthor of *The Prosperity Paradox: How Innovation Can Lift Nations Out of Poverty* (HarperCollins, 2019).

JAMES DE VRIES is the owner and director of de Luxe & Associates and the former creative director of the Harvard Business Review Group.

KAREN DILLON is the former editor of *Harvard Business Review* and a coauthor of *The Prosperity Paradox: How Innovation Can Lift Nations Out of Poverty* (HarperCollins, 2019).

DAVID S. DUNCAN is a senior partner at Innosight. He is a coauthor of *Competing Against Luck: The Story of Innovation and Customer Choice* (HarperBusiness/HarperCollins, October 2016).

AMY C. EDMONDSON is the Novartis Professor of Leadership and Management at Harvard Business School. She is the author of *The Fearless Organization: Creating Psychological Safety in the Workplace for Learning, Innovation, and Growth* (Wiley, 2019) and a coauthor of *Building the Future: Big Teaming for Audacious Innovation* (Berrett-Koehler, 2016).

VIJAY GOVINDARAJAN is the Coxe Distinguished Professor at Dartmouth College's Tuck School of Business. He is the lead author of *The Three-Box Solution* and *The Three-Box Solution Playbook*.

TADDY HALL is a principal with the Cambridge Group and the leader of Nielsen's Breakthrough Innovation Project. He is a coauthor of *Competing Against Luck: The Story of Innovation and Customer Choice* (HarperBusiness/HarperCollins, October 2016).

ADI IGNATIUS is editor in chief of *Harvard Business Review*.

DAVID KELLEY is the founder and chairman of IDEO and the founder of the Hasso Plattner Institute of Design at Stanford, where he is the Donald W. Whittier Professor in Mechanical Engineering.

TOM KELLEY is the coauthor of *Creative Confidence* (Crown Business, 2013) and a partner at IDEO, a global design and innovation firm.

JEANNE M. LIEDTKA is a professor at the University of Virginia's Darden School of Business.

ROGER L. MARTIN is the director of the Martin Prosperity Institute and a former dean of the Rotman School of Management at the University of Toronto. He is a coauthor of *Creating Great Choices: A Leader's Guide to Integrative Thinking* (Harvard Business Review Press, 2017).

INDRA NOOYI is the former chairman and CEO of PepsiCo.

CAROLINE O'CONNOR is a lecturer at the Hasso Plattner Institute of Design.

MAURO PORCINI is PepsiCo's chief design officer—the first to hold the position—where he oversees design-led innovation across all of the company's brands.

SARAH STEIN GREENBERG is the managing director of the Hasso Plattner Institute of Design.

AMOS WINTER is the Robert N. Noyce Career Development Assistant Professor and the director of the Global Engineering and Research Laboratory in the department of mechanical engineering at the Massachusetts Institute of Technology.

Index